1776...
A COMPLETELY NEW AND CONVINCING
PROOF OF GOD

1776...

A COMPLETELY NEW AND CONVINCING

PROOF OF GOD

CONTAINING MANY NEWLY DISCOVERED AND CONVINCING EVIDENCES FOR THE EXISTENCE AND POWER OF GOD, USING ONLY THE DIGITS OF PI AND THE LAW OF PROBABILITY.

LLOYD STRAPPINI

ISBN: 978-1-0683384-1-0
Paperback edition

This is the first published edition of
1776... A Completely New and Convincing Proof of God
by Lloyd Strappini.

Also available in e-book format.

Printed in the United Kingdom
Formatting and design by UK Design Co.

PROLOGUE

The Pi Encryption is a standing, undeniable, unshakeable, testable, ever-present and enduring testimony of the truth of Christ's claims concerning His deity and the salvation that He alone can give to every soul who will trust in Him.

It has only been discovered in recent years, by the use of 21st century technology.

Phenomena like the **Pi Encryption** do not "just happen" by themselves – at least, not in the real world.

This book is the means by which it is being made public **for the very first time**.

Until now, no one – *no one at all* – has *ever* been able to find even a simple and meaningless pattern in π, let alone a complex one that conveys *detailed information.*

BUT NOW, FOR THE FIRST TIME, WE HAVE

THE PI ENCRYPTION!

CONTENTS

APPENDICES:

PREFACE

JUST TRY TO IMAGINE that you have an extremely important Message to convey – a Message that can only be expressed by encrypting [(1)] three numbers: **386, 888** and **86.**

AND that you have an infinite number of figures (the digits of π) in which to convey it.

And **JUST IMAGINE** (if you can) that you are omnipotent.

How will you go about doing this?

Having regard to the intended recipients of the Message (21st century humans), you know that, as digital technology will be available to them, they will be able to search through several billion digits of π without too much difficulty.

Even so, in order to ensure that the Message is well within their reach, you decide that it should be hidden somewhere near the *beginning* of π, where, at the appointed time, it will be relatively easy for them to find.

You will need to choose a specific short section of π in which to hide it, as otherwise the Message will be too spread out and hard to find.

Now **JUST IMAGINE** that the place where you choose to start constructing the encryption is the 23,000,000 digits in π starting at decimal place number 100,000,001 and ending at decimal place number 123,000,000.

One reason for choosing this particular section of π could be that 23,000,000 breaks down easily into three sections, each of which neatly expresses a key element (**386**, **888** or **86**) of the planned encryption, as shown in table 1 on the next page.

TABLE 1

	Number of decimal places	Significance
FIRST SECTION (17,772,000 decimal places)	17,766,772	twice **888**$_3$**386**
	2,614	**386** inverted*
	2,614	**386** inverted* (N.B. the total number of decimal places in the first section is 17,772,000, or twice 8886000, a conflation of **888** and **86**)
SECOND SECTION (2,614,000 decimal places)	2,614,000	**386** inverted*
THIRD SECTION (2,614,000 decimal places)	2,614,000	**386** inverted*
	Total: 23,000,000	

*for an explanation of inversions, see chapter 8

We now have a very basic framework.

Having established this basic framework, three simple (and extremely small) adjustments will need to be made:

ADJUSTMENT 1 -	increase the First section (and with it the total length of the basic framework) by 4,065 decimal places;
ADJUSTMENT 2 -	remove 900 decimal places from the Second section (reducing it from 2,614,000 to 2,613,100) and transfer them to the First section; and
ADJUSTMENT 3 -	remove a further 900 decimal places from the Third section (reducing it also from 2,614,000 to 2,613,100) and transfer them to the First section.

(It is noteworthy that Adjustments 2 and 3, being identical, are evidence of a *consistent* and *systematic* approach).

With these three tiny adjustments [(2)], the outer boundaries and two of the main internal divisions of "**The Encryption Zone**" (as it is named in this book) are now firmly and permanently established, as shown in table 2 on page xvi.

It is necessary now to mark out the "**Key Points**" of the **Zone**, without which it will be impossible for anyone to decipher the hidden Message.

There are four of these, the first and last of which (**Key Points A** and **D**) mark the outer boundaries of the **Zone.**

The third (**Key Point C**) is at the precise boundary between the **<u>Second</u>** and **<u>Third Adjusted Sections</u>**.

But the second (**Key Point B**) is at a totally new position, calibrated with such extraordinary precision that it defines and pinpoints, in combination with each of the other three **Key Points**,

TABLE 2

	Number of decimal places	Significance
ADJUSTED FIRST SECTION	17,766,772	twice **8883386**
	2,614	**386** inverted*
	2,614	**386** inverted*
(as adjusted by Adjustments 1, 2 and 3)	4,065	(added by Adjustment 1)
	900	transferred from the **Second Section** by Adjustment 2.
	900	transferred from the **Third Section** by Adjustment 3. (17,777,865 is now the total number of decimal places in the **Adjusted First Section**)
ADJUSTED SECOND SECTION (as adjusted by Adjustment 2)	2,613,100	(2,614,000 minus the 900 decimal places transferred to the **First Section** by Adjustment 1)
ADJUSTED THIRD SECTION (as adjusted by Adjustment 3)	2,613,100	(2,614,000 minus the 900 decimal places transferred to the **First Section** by Adjustment 2)
Total:	23,004,065	π digits 100,000,001 to 123,004,065 inclusive –"**the Encryption Zone**".

*for an explanation of inversions, see chapter 8

the exact position not only of all 4 of them, but also of the boundaries between the **First**, **Second**, and **Third Adjusted Sections**. (3)

And finally, it is necessary to establish a **key** to the **Pi Encryption**, without which its all-important Message would remain hidden forever.

But you will have to read a little further on to find out what it is!

Notes on the Preface

(1) Some may object that it is not in God's character to conceal (in this case by encryption) the good gifts of His Providence; yet both the Old and the New Testaments contain passages which clearly affirm the opposite:

"It is the glory of God to conceal a thing: but the honour of kings is to search out a matter" (Proverbs 25:2); and

"And his disciples asked him, saying, What might this parable be? And he said, Unto you it is given to know the mysteries of the Kingdom of God: but to others in parables; that seeing they might not see and hearing they might not understand" (Luke 8: 9-10).

(2) This sub-division of the Encryption Zone is fully validated by, among other things, the appearance of the length of the Adjusted First Section (17,777,865) as an essential component in no fewer than 9 of the 14 "Secret Pathways" discussed in chapter 22.

(3) All of this will be explained later.

A GLOSSARY OF TERMS

Alter ego	A second self.
Average	An amount obtained by dividing the total of given amounts by the number of amounts in the set.*
Binomial calculator	A calculator that computes probabilities according to their binomial distribution.
Binomial distribution	a frequency distribution of the possible number of successful outcomes in a given number of trials in each of which there is the same probability of success.*
Correspondence	is where a sequence of digits in Pi corresponds in a significant way to the decimal place numbers in Pi at which the sequence is found.
Decimal Fraction	A fraction whose denominator is a power of ten, especially when expressed positionally by units to the right of a decimal point (e.g., 0.2, 0.0005, 0.141592, etc.).*
Digit	Any of the 10 numerals from 0 – 9 inclusive.
Digits Between	The number of decimal places separating two points in the decimal expansion of π. See chapter 20.
Digits of Pi	The digits which together make up π. See chapter 20.

Encryption Zone The string of 23,004,065 digits in π, starting at decimal place number 100,000,001 and finishing at decimal place number 123,004,065, where the Pi Encryption is to be found.

Exact Accurate to within one digit or decimal place.

Feature One of the 37 observations, statistical anomalies, or patterns, forming part of the Pi Encryption, which have been selected for inclusion in this book.

First Section The First Section of the Encryption Zone, comprising decimal place numbers 100,000,001 to 17,777,865 inclusive, as explained in the Preface.

Golden Pathway An interlocking pattern which connects all four Key Points together with pinpoint accuracy. See chapter 11.

Hallmark of Design A phenomenon the orderly characteristics of which are rationally inconsistent with having been generated by a random process.

Inversion The expression of a number by what is left when it is subtracted from a higher multiple of 1,000 (e.g. 614 for 386); or, in the case of a decimal fraction, from 1. See chapter 8.

Jesus Magnification A pattern, innate in the structure of Pi, whereby the length of the Encryption Zone (23,004,065) represents, with great accuracy, the ratio between the numerical values of the name "Jesus" expressed in Hebrew and Greek. See chapter 14.

Key Point One of the four points in Pi on which the Pi Encryption is founded. See chapter 6.

Key to the Pi Encryption	The number 17766771, which is effectively the key combination needed to unlock the secrets of the Pi Encryption. See chapter 10.
Ordinal	Defining a thing's position in a series*.
Palindrome	A word, phrase, or string of digits, which reads the same both forwards and backwards. See chapter 10.
Palindromic law	The rule that any sequence of letters or digits that does not read exactly the same forwards and backwards, is not a palindrome.
Pattern	A relationship or connection between two or more numbers or strings of numbers which, whether by reason of symmetry, value, consistency, balance, accuracy, sequence, proportionality, system, placing, or the apparent existence of a common underlying plan, scheme, theme or process, should rationally be interpreted as a hallmark of design.
Pi (π)	The name commonly given to the ratio between the circumference of a circle and its diameter.
Pi Encryption	The encryption (in the form of multiple mathematical patterns) of the name "Jesus" which is found in the section of Pi referred to in this book as "the Encryption Zone".
Pinpoint precision	Accuracy to within one digit or decimal place.
Probability	The extent to which an event is likely to occur, measured by the ratio of the favourable cases to the whole number of cases possible.*
Remainder	A number left after division or subtraction.*

Second Section The Second Section of the Encryption Zone, comprising the 2,613,100 decimal places from number 17,777,866 to number 120,390,965 inclusive, as explained in the Preface.

Shortfall A deficit below what was expected.*

Step factor One of a limited number of whole numbers by which a sum must be modified (usually by multiplication or division), in order to pass from one step to the next in the computation of a pattern forming part of the Pi Encryption. The only step factors accepted as valid in this book are 2,4,5,10 (and multiples of any of these with 10), and 7.

Third Section The Third Section of the Encryption Zone, comprising the 2,613,100 decimal places from number 120,390,966 to number 123,004,065 inclusive, as explained in the Preface.

*as defined in the Oxford English Dictionary

INTRODUCTION

AN UNUSUAL GIFT

How this began.

If you open a text book on mathematics, you will find that the expression "π" (which is the Greek letter for "p", often written in English as "pi"), is the name given to the relationship between the circumference of a circle (the distance around its edge) and its diameter (the distance across its middle).

It is thought to have first come into use in 1706, as shorthand for "Periphery" (1).

You can calculate the distance around the edge of a circle by multiplying its diameter by Pi, a number which never ends (in other words, it is infinite) but which starts off with 3.141592. (2)

As I have no formal training as a mathematician, and this book deals, in large measure, with a mathematical topic, for me to begin writing it is very daunting indeed.

Daunting, because my task is to persuade my readers of the existence of something which, by all conventional wisdom (including, as far as I know, the universal opinion of the entire mathematical community), simply should not be there at all - an elegant and complex network of interlocking patterns, or designs, embedded within the very structure of the decimal expansion of Pi!

Patterns that carry, encrypted within them, a message of the most immense importance to every man, woman and child on planet Earth.

Having regard to the above, it seems clear that I should not invite you to read a book of this kind without first giving you a brief insight into its background.

Some years ago Mike, a client of my legal firm (and a committed Christian), strode purposefully into my office, and, without saying a word, placed a book (3) on my desk, before turning on his heels and leaving, with no more than a meaningful glance in my direction.

"Odd behaviour", you may think.

And you would be right!

(But, after all, "odd behaviour" should sometimes be expected of Gospel believers, if they are walking in obedience).

When I examined the book, I found it to be an altogether unexpected introduction to a field of study I knew next to nothing about - Bible numbers.

The idea behind the book - that the Bible contained numerical codes - seemed so bizarre as to belong to the world of fantasy, rather than fact.

And yet, what if…?

I had always had a bit of a taste for unusual ideas and theories, and the idea struck a chord deep down within.

Besides, as the book had come to me as a gift, it would have been ungrateful not to give it a glance.

It was clearly not a recent publication, the first edition having been printed well before I was born.

Its name, style and layout all seemed to hark back to a bygone age, more like an old-fashioned religious tract than a book one would read for relaxation.

However, as I turned its pages, the conviction grew within me that there was much more to all this than I could ever have thought possible.

There followed years of interest in the field - though pursued somewhat intermittently, it must be said, through pressure of work, and life generally.

My interest deepened to the point where I started to make investigations of my own, mostly in the Old Testament Book of Isaiah.

But in many ways the most compelling evidence I have come across is not to be found in the Bible at all, but in the natural world of mathematics - and specifically in the decimal expansion of Pi.

It is that evidence which forms the subject-matter of this book.

I do hope you will enjoy reading about the **Pi Encryption** as much as I have enjoyed discovering and writing about it.

<u>**Notes on the introduction**</u>

(1) In the book by the distinguished Welsh mathematician William Jones (1675-1749) entitled "Synopsis Palmariorum Matheseos: or, a New Introduction to the Mathematics", London, 1706, pp. 243 and 263.

(2) However, if you do this, as you must, using a finite number of π digits, your result will always be slightly short of the true answer, because π is infinite.

(3) "The Seal of God in Creation and the Word" by F.C. Payne, 10th edition (1969).

CHAPTER 1

"BEYOND REASONABLE DOUBT"

Our quest is to find strong, objective and convincing new evidence for the truth of the Christian Faith, of such a nature as should be sufficient to convince a trial jury "beyond reasonable doubt".

Some years ago, I spoke about my faith in Jesus to a professional colleague of mine, a lawyer with something of a reputation as a formidable opponent.

Her somewhat startling response was that she would only accept the Christian Gospel if I could prove it to her "beyond reasonable doubt"!

For readers who are unfamiliar with that phrase, it describes the very high standard of proof that the prosecutor has to satisfy, in a criminal case, in order to obtain a conviction.

In other words, the members of the jury, before they can return a verdict of guilty, must be convinced by the evidence they have heard to such a high degree that they feel sure of the accused person's guilt, "beyond reasonable doubt".

On hearing this, I realised that my colleague was expressing a deep resistance to the Gospel, and that she would be unlikely to consider putting her faith in the Lord Jesus Christ - at least for the time being!

Reflecting on her words, I knew of no way that Christianity could ever be proved *objectively*, as one does in a court room, to anything approaching that high standard of proof – "beyond reasonable doubt".

This is because the evidence for Christianity, though extremely abundant, is largely *subjective* in nature, depending, as it does, on the deep personal convictions and experiences of the particular Christians who happen to be testifying to it.

A non-Christian hearing such testimony can invariably shrug it off as no more than an expression of the speaker's personal background, beliefs and preferences, which can safely be ignored by a person (such as the hearer often presumes himself to be) of higher intellect and superior understanding.

The external and objective proofs, and in particular the inferences to be drawn from the wonders of the natural world, have today, at least for many of us, been unjustly robbed of much of their power by naturalistic interpretations of biology.

My quest since then has been to find a way to prove the truth of Christianity, to such a high standard that even the most antagonistic of non-Christians (if they are open to reason) will be given serious pause for reflection.

The need for such a proof has become increasingly urgent, in recent decades, with the growing popularity of a virulent strain of militant atheism.

In this book I will attempt to present, as clearly as possible, the objectively demonstrable evidence that I have found in support of the truth of the Christian Gospel.

The Bible will not be relied on at all, for if I did so those who are opposed to the Gospel would condemn this as circular argumentation.

Indeed, every shred of evidence presented here can be checked, tested and exposed to as much rational scrutiny and appraisal as is necessary, to satisfy the doubting mind.

My core policy throughout has been to massively *understate* the case for God, and to massively *overstate* the case against Him, as to do otherwise would inevitably lead to accusations of exaggeration.

I have done my best to be truthful and accurate in every detail. Your own personal conclusions - your verdict – will be for you alone to decide.

But please remember that the mathematical features presented in this book have been deliberately arranged in ascending order, starting with the least, and moving steadily towards those with greater probative force. For this reason, don't be surprised if you find some of the earlier features somewhat underwhelming. It is important that you read to the very end, in order to gain the full impact of all the evidence.

I wish you every pleasure, and success, in completing the journey that lies ahead.

CHAPTER 2

THE MIGHTY NAME OF JESUS

How the most exalted name of Jesus, just like any lesser name, can be expressed in numbers.

We have to start with the name of Jesus.

When I have finished explaining, you will see why it is fundamental to everything.

It is a little-known fact that the name "Jesus" (like any other word) can be expressed both in writing (using letters of the alphabet), and numerically (using figures).

This is because, in ancient times, the two languages in which most (1) of the Bible was originally written, Hebrew and Greek, had no separate system of numbers.

Instead, the Hebrews and Greeks used letters of their alphabets to express numbers.

In Hebrew, their equivalent of "a" (alef) represented 1, their "b" (bet), 2, and so on.

In Greek, their "a" (alpha) represented 1, their "b" (beta), 2, and so on.

Thus, every group of Hebrew or Greek characters written down on a page can be read either as a series of letters of the alphabet, or numerically, as a string of digits.

By adding together the numerical values of the letters of a person's name, one arrives at the numerical value of that name (2).

This applies to everyone, including Jesus.

There are two appendices near the end of this book, setting out the numerical values of the letters of the Hebrew and Greek languages [(3)].

There are also some other appendices showing how the numerical values used in this book are arrived at[(4)].

Please refer to them if you need to check anything.

Expressed numerically, the name "Jesus" is **386** in Hebrew and **888** in Greek [(5)].

As these two values are fundamental to everything that follows, please pause for a moment to take them in and memorise them.

386 and **888** are quite simply the most important numbers in the universe.

And as you read on, you will see exactly why.

Notes to chapter 2

(1) Parts of the Old Testament books of Ezra, Daniel and Jeremiah were written in Aramaic, and the New Testament also contains some short passages in that language, though written in Greek letters.

(2) A very well known Biblical example of this is to be found in Revelation 13.18: "Here is wisdom. Let him that hath understanding count the number of the beast: for it is the number of a man; and his number is six hundred threescore and six".

(3) See Appendix 1 and Appendix 2.

(4) See Appendix 3 (**386** - "Jesus"), Appendix 4 (**888** - "Jesus"), and Appendix 5 (**86** - "God").

(5) For how these are calculated, see Appendices 3 and 4.

CHAPTER 3

AN "UNBELIEVABLE" TRUTH

How can the name "Jesus" possibly be the basis for complex numerical patterns in π?

As far as anyone knows, the decimal expansion of Pi goes on forever.

Although in modern times it has been calculated to trillions of decimal places, there is absolutely no sign that the end of it will ever be found.

In fact, it is the universal belief of mathematicians that it has no end.(1)

In this sense, Christians could say that it is like God(2).

Another opinion universally held among mathematicians is that there are no patterns in Pi, except such as occur purely at random and are therefore meaningless.

To try to see meaning in such *randomly generated* patterns would be as nonsensical as "reading" a person's tea leaves, or gazing into a crystal ball.

But what if patterns could be found that *could not* have been generated randomly, but *must* have originated in someone's mind?

It is the "unbelievable" claim of this book that many patterns of the utmost intricacy, meaning and design, do indeed exist within π, all of them firmly and unmistakably based on the numerical expressions of the name of Jesus - **386** and **888**(3).

An astonishing claim, but one which is actually true – yes *really!*

Please suspend your disbelief until you have read through to the end of this book. If you keep a genuinely open mind, you may reap a rich and eternal reward.

At the end, *but only at the end*, decide for yourself whether you can honestly reject this book's claims.

There is a great deal of completely new, and deeply challenging, evidence ahead of you.

<u>And you will need to keep a truly open mind in order to be able to reach a sound verdict, like a trial jury, based *only* on the evidence which will be placed before you.</u>

<u>Notes to chapter 3</u>

(1) In 1770, Swiss mathematician Johann Heinrich Lambert proved Pi to be an "irrational" number (that is, a real number that cannot be represented as a simple fraction). As such, its decimal expansion must be infinite, as is the case with all irrational numbers.

(2) How fitting therefore, Christians might claim, if God chose to use it as a way of displaying His power and majesty.

(3) For an explanation of **<u>386</u>** and **<u>888</u>**, see chapter 2.

CHAPTER 4

SOME PRELIMINARY REFLECTIONS ON THE PI ENCRYPTION

How *impossible* this all is - yet real!

The **Pi Encryption** is a phenomenon of such immense beauty, power and significance, that it quite literally defies description - like a majestic cathedral, built to inspire awe and worship.

Its principal pillars, beams, arches and vaults are not made of wood or stone, but of a substance infinitely more durable and sure [(1)].

So finely balanced and exquisitely crafted is the fabric of this vast edifice, and so heavily dependent is it on the name and integrity of its Great Master Builder, that if any part of it were ever to be removed or replaced, (even by the merest fraction of a decimal place), the whole would need to be recast anew, to accommodate the change.

For if a single digit of Pi were altered (if that were possible!) all the remaining digits, both before and after it, must also be altered.

But, if changed, the result would no longer be Pi – for, just as a circle can never be anything but a circle, so Pi can never be anything but Pi.

So the Builder of this sublime structure must have had an overview of the infinite whole, and equal and simultaneous sovereignty over each and every part of it, and a computing power transcendent over infinity.

And, in the process of its conception, each tiny adjustment, wherever and however it occurred, must necessarily have been simultaneously accompanied by an infinite number of correlative compensating adjustments, in every other part.

And, given the essential immutability of Pi, these patterns must have been there from the very beginning - and even from before the beginning.

Exhibiting pinpoint accuracy, over boundless millions of decimal places; unlimited in space and time; necessarily conformable to the substance and properties of the circle - yet somehow, at the same time, conveying a clear and unmistakable message – though in a medium by which no *human* mind can conceive that a message is capable of being conveyed.

Can we agree, before we even start to examine it, that such an edifice would be a most breathtaking and superlative wonder - a marvel beyond belief, transporting us, quite literally, into the realm of the impossible –

Yet an "impossible" made real before our very eyes!

Notes to chapter 4

(1) They are these: **86** ("God" in Hebrew), **386** ("Jesus" in Hebrew), **888** (Jesus" in Greek), and the four **Key Points** (see chapter 6).

CHAPTER 5

DISCOVERIES BEGIN

How the key to the **Pi Encryption** - **17766771** - first came into view.

Some time ago, I became interested in Pi.

I wondered whether there were any patterns in it which might open up, and throw light on, deeper truths.

In the course of my research, I came across an internet website (1) offering easy π searches from the first decimal place after the decimal point to place number 200,000,000.

I used that website extensively in the early stages of my inquiries, which produced some interesting results.

But the greatest breakthrough came unexpectedly, when I set the website's search engine to find the digit-sequence **17766771**, which I had no reason, at that time, to think of as having anything special about it, except that it was a palindrome formed out of **1,776** (twice **888**, "Jesus" in Greek) - one **1776** going forwards and another **1776** going backwards - **1776** and **6771**, or **17766771**.

According to theory (as later confirmed by my research) (2), any given eight digit sequence, such as **17766771**, can be reasonably expected to occur in Pi, on average, only once in every 100,000,000 digits.

In fact, the sequence **17766771** only occurs 34 times in the first four and a half billion digits of Pi, an average frequency of about once per 132,000,000 places.

And yet, despite an expected average frequency of only 1 in 100,000,000, I found that the first three occurrences of **17766771** are in fact all crammed into a tiny section of Pi, less than twenty million decimal places long, starting not far after the hundred millionth place, as follows:

The **first** occurrence of **17766771** starts at position	103,227,186
The **second** occurrence of **17766771** starts at position	120,390,965
The **third** occurrence of **17766771** starts at position	123,004,065

The probability of such a close-knit cluster as this occurring anywhere in Pi *by pure chance* would seem, by any reasonable standard, to be very low [5].

But what makes it particularly intriguing, as a striking statistical anomaly, is that it occurs so very close to the beginning of Pi, [3][5] at a point which is relatively easy for us human beings, using 21st century technology, to find and study.

It is as if it has been deliberately placed there - near the beginning - as a sign to us all, at this specific time in history, that there is a wonderful treasure to be found, just under the surface, for those who will dig down to find it.

My interest aroused, I found that the distance from the first occurrence to the third was exactly **1**9776879 decimal places [4][5] (incorporating **1,776**, which is twice **888**, "Jesus" in Greek, within it), and that half of **1**9776879 is 9**888**439.5 ("Jesus" in Greek [5])!

The chance of all this happening randomly, I reasoned, could not be high.

Already, this was beginning to look very interesting indeed.

But I could not have imagined, at that early stage, just how fascinating it would become!

This book presents the main discoveries made during a long voyage of exploration, the likes of which, I sincerely believe, have never been recorded before.

For me, the Pi Encryption has been a "once in a lifetime" discovery, and my hope is that it will be the same for you, too.

Notes to chapter 5

(1) "The Pi Search Page", http://www.angio.net/pi/piquery I later had my own search engine constructed to enable me to search the first 4,500,000,000 (four and a half billion) digits of Pi – see note 2 below.

(2) The empirical method I adopted was to use a bespoke search engine, which I had installed on my computer, to count how many times each one of a trial set of 2,500 *randomly selected* eight digit sequences occurred in the first 4,500,000,000 digits of Pi. Of the sample of 2,500 I investigated, the sequence with the lowest number of occurrences was 07321010, with only 25, and the one with the largest number was 65280440, with 72. The average number of appearances of all 2,500 eight-digit sequences I investigated was 44.952, indicating an average frequency in Pi for all 8 digit sequences of 1 per 100,000,000; (i.e. as the average number of appearances in 4,500,000,000 digits is 44.952, the average incidence of appearances is almost exactly 1 per 100,000,000, assuming a random distribution). This is of considerable interest, because it proves that although π is obviously not random (otherwise it could not be calculated), the frequency and distribution of its digits appear to be generally indistinguishable from what one would expect to find if it were (thus, incidentally, making the existence of the **Pi Encryption** even more remarkable).

(3) This nearness of the **Encryption Zone** to the beginning of Pi – starting just over 100,000,000 decimal places from the start and making it relatively easy to find with the help of 21st century technology - is in fact a very important feature of the **Pi Encryption**, because, in an infinite series such as π is believed to be, it is arguable that all patterns that are capable of occurring will in fact occur an infinite number of times. The further away from the start of π any pattern forming part of the **Pi Encryption** occurred, therefore, the more plausible it would be to argue that it had arisen by mere chance, and not by design, as the larger the number of digits preceding it, the larger the number of past, unsuccessful, opportunities for it to have formed randomly.

(4) As **17766771** is the common factor identifying the two positions in Pi between which the measurement of 19776879 was taken, this find hints strongly at an amazing interrelationship between the locations in Pi where a given string of digits may be found, and the digits composing the string itself. As you read on, you will find, seemingly contrary to all logic and reason, that the connection is real (being confirmed in many different ways), and far from unique. Please refer in particular to chapter 20.

(5) All the noteworthy points reported in this chapter – the close-knit clustering of the first three occurrences in Pi of **17766771**, their nearness to the beginning of Pi, and the characteristics of 19776879 listed above, will, in the interests of avoiding any suspicion of exaggeration, be grouped together, for the purposes of this book, as though they were only one - "Feature 1" – thus substantially *handicapping* the case for design being made in this book.

(6) **Hallmarks of Design in chapter 5**

The statistically improbable clustering together of the first three occurrences in Pi of the digit string **17766771** is an example of **significant grouping**.

The fact that the first and the third of them, both instances of **17766771**, are divided from each other by **1**9776879 decimal places, evinces **correspondence** between the actual digits of Pi and the place-numbers where they occur.

The repeated occurrence of **1776** (2 x 888) endows this whole pattern with a message (**information and meaning**) - the name of Jesus.

This message is profoundly **consistent** with that conveyed throughout this book - the name and divine nature of Jesus.

CHAPTER 6

THE FOUR KEY POINTS

An introduction to the four principal points in π on which the **Pi Encryption** is founded.

1. Introduction

As you read through this book, you will be struck time and time again by the fact that the relatively short section of Pi starting at place-number 100,000,001, and ending at place-number 123,004,065 (called in this book **"the Encryption Zone"**) is a very real unit, distinct unto itself, and infused with many totally unique and extraordinary qualities and characteristics.

What sets it apart from the rest of π, and unites it internally, is the large number of numerical patterns and designs which run all the way through it - patterns and designs which I have grouped together, for the purpose of this book, under the general title **"the Pi Encryption"**(1).

When describing and discussing these patterns and designs, it is convenient, and indeed necessary, for us to find a shorthand means of referring to their most prominent features, as these are the bedrock of the **Encryption**, and will crop up repeatedly in every chapter as we go on.

2. The Four Key Points

The four most basic and essential points, which we shall encounter over and over again, will be referred to in this book as **Key Points A**, **B**, **C** and **D**:-

- **KEY POINT A** is decimal place number **100,000,000**, which marks the end of the section of π immediately preceding the **Encryption Zone**, the first decimal place of which is therefore number 100,000,001 (2);
- **KEY POINT B** is decimal place number **103,227,186**, the *first* occurrence in π of the digit-sequence **17766771**;
- **KEY POINT C** is decimal place number **120,390,965**, the *second* occurrence in π of the digit-sequence **17766771**; and
- **KEY POINT D** is decimal place number **123,004,065**, the *third* occurrence in π of the digit-sequence **17766771**.

Although there is nothing very special to distinguish them on the surface, the more closely we study these four Key Points, the more you will come to see just how extraordinary they really are.

3. A point to note and remember

Before we go on to the next chapter, I think I should make an important point, although it is one that may seem obvious to many of you.

If patterns come into existence in nature (some would say "randomly"), as with whirlpools in a fast-flowing river, shimmering sunlight on the surface of the sea, a rainbow, or the intricate crystal shape of a snowflake, they will never be restricted to an artificially defined part of the river, sea or atmosphere, but will always, of necessity, be liable to appear *wherever* all the natural conditions that are needed to form them *happen* to exist.

Similarly, spiders' webs will occur wherever there *happen* to be web-forming spiders, weaver bird nests wherever weaver birds *happen* to breed, etc.

But the patterns and designs of the **Pi Encryption** are not only focused and centred on the **Encryption Zone**, but actually do not work at all (in the case of many of them) unless you completely eliminate everything that precedes the **Zone** - the whole of the first 100,000,000 digits of Pi - by subtracting **Key Point A** - 100,000,000 - from the other three **Key Points,** before you proceed any further with the calculation!

Yet there is no logical reason to believe that those first 100,000,000 decimal places (or indeed any of those following the **Zone**) are any less *naturally* favourable, or suitable, for the formation of such phenomena, than those within it(3).

This, as an obvious hallmark of design(4), is an extremely powerful argument for the divine origin of the **Pi Encryption**.

One which I make at this early stage, because you will undoubtedly wish to reflect carefully upon it as you read through the following chapters, and become acquainted with the many individual features of the **Pi Encryption**.

Notes to chapter 6

(1) Although the expression selected for use is in the singular – "The Pi Encryption" – a strong case could be made for using the plural, as each of the 37 "features" described in this book is effectively a separate and independent witness of the Divine Name being encrypted in Pi. However, allowing oneself to get too bogged down in such minutiae would risk obscuring the real point – that, whatever one makes of the **Pi Encryption**, it simply could not have "just happened" by itself!

(2) Some readers may object that decimal place number 100,000,000 should not be given the designation "**Key Point A**", as that name should be reserved for 103,227,186, the *first* occurrence in π of the digit string **17766771**. In support of their objection, they may argue that the letter "A" is usually, and rightly, associated with the *first* in a series. However, although decimal place number 100,000,000 does not mark the first (or indeed any) occurrence of **17766771**, it is, undoubtedly, an essential element in the **Pi Encryption**, as is proved by the frequent and crucial part it plays in many of the patterns featured in the following chapters. Another possible objection to 100,000,000 being designated "**Key Point A**" is that (unlike the other three Key Points) it is not itself to be found within the **Encryption Zone**, the first decimal place of which is actually the one immediately following it, number 100,000,001. But, in my view, these objections are nothing more than "splitting hairs". As it is 100,000,000, (and not 100,000,001), that has to be subtracted from the other **Key Points** as a necessary step in forming many of the patterns featured in the following chapters, its designation as "**Key Point A**" is, in this author's opinion, not only fully justified, but logically inevitable.

(3) This is not to say that there are no significant patterns at all, in π, outside of the **Encryption Zone**. For instance, as the first occurrence in π of the digit-sequence 1776 (twice 888, "Jesus") starts at decimal place number 889, it follows that there are exactly 888 ("Jesus") decimal places preceding it, (meaning that the first 888 decimal places in π are demarcated from the second by the sum of them both – 1776) – a very neat and pleasing pattern indeed, *yet not found within the Encryption Zone.*

(4) And also as one of the signature "*modi operandi*" of the designer of the Pi Encryption, along with inversions (see chapter 8), correspondences (see chapter 20 among many others) and combination codes (see chapter 21).

CHAPTER 7

SCRATCHING AT THE SURFACE

Some relatively "on the surface" examples of patterns in the **Pi Encryption**.

On noticing the strange clustering of the first three occurrences in Pi of the digit-sequence **17766771**, and the other surface features described in chapter 5, I decided to take a closer look.

What I was particularly interested in finding was any further evidence of patterns based on either **386** or **888**.

And any occurrences of **86** ("God" in Hebrew) would also be of obvious importance.

Any connection between **386**, **888** or **86** and **Key Points A**, **B**, **C** and **D** would be of extreme interest.

As I had no idea of the existence of inversions [(1)], I was not looking for them yet, at that early stage.

But, even without them, I soon found that if one first subtracts **Key Point A** (the first 100,000,000 digits of Pi) [(2)] [(3)]:

- **Key Point C** stands in a relation of roughly 0.**888** ("Jesus" in Greek) to **Key Point D**[(4)] ;and;
- **Key Point D** multiplied by 0.**386** ("Jesus" in Hebrew) comes to **888**0,000 ("Jesus" in Greek)[(5)].

FURTHERMORE the distance between **Key Points B** and **D**, expressed as a fraction of the whole length of the **Encryption Zone**, is 0.**86** ("God" in Hebrew) (6);

AND MOREOVER, adding together all the digits of the first three places in Pi of the sequence **17766771** comes to a total of **86** ("God" in Hebrew), as follows:

Key Point B		**Key Point C**		**Key Point D**	
1+0+3+2+2+7+1+8+6	+	1+2+0+3+9+0+9+6+5	+	1+2+3+0+0+4+0+6+5	= **86**
103227186		120390965		123004065	

AND FINALLY, we should not overlook the small but significant fact that **Key Point B** ends with an **86** (1032271**86**).

These minor and (I admit) relatively unimpressive points(7) will, I hope, serve to set a modest stage for the many much greater, and more spectacular, wonders to be described in the later chapters of this book.

For we are still only just beginning to "scratch at the surface" of God's wonderful **Pi Encryption**.

Notes to chapter 7

(1) See chapter 8.

(2) It is worth noting here that the systematic and repeated subtraction of any number (in this case, 100,000,000), from a group of other numbers, before combining the remainders together in various ways in the manner described here, is a sure sign of method and order, which of course are attributes not of chaos or chance, but of an intelligent and creative mind.

(3) In fact, all three of the following results show slight margins of difference from the values attributed to them in the text. However, these are so small as to be negligible for the present ("scratching at the surface") purposes. They are indicated by "±" notations in notes 4, 5 and 6.

(4) **20,390,965** ÷ **23,004,065** = 0.**888** (± 0.001592).

(5) **23,004,065** x 0.**386** = **888**0,000 (± 430.90).

(6) The distance between **Key Points B** and **D** is 19,776,879, and the whole length of the **Encryption Zone** is **23,004,065**. Therefore 19,776,879 divided by **23,004,065** is 0.**86** (+ 0.0002876).

(7) In the interests of avoiding any suspicion of exaggeration, all the noteworthy features reported in this chapter will be grouped together, for the purposes of this book, as if there were only one -"Feature 2" – thus substantially handicapping the case for design which I am placing before you.

(8) **Hallmarks of Design in chapter 7.**

The first three of the points noted in this chapter all result from the initial application of an identical **system or process**, requiring **Key Point A** (100,000,000) to be subtracted from **Key Point D** (123,004,065), so as to leave the length of the **Encryption Zone** (23,004,065), before the rest of the calculation is completed.

Each of them demonstrates **accuracy** to an astonishingly high degree, conveys **information and meaning** in the words "God" and "Jesus", and in so doing evinces remarkable **consistency**.

Finally, the fact that the sum of the digits in **Key Points B**, **C** and **D** (86) reflects with uncanny **accuracy**, not only the Hebrew word for God (86), but also the ratio between the distance from **Key Point B** to **Key Point D** (19,776,879) and the whole length of the Encryption Zone (23,004,065), manifests striking **correspondence** between the name of God and the Key elements of the **Encryption Zone**.

CHAPTER 8

INVERSIONS

How the quantity of air there is in a wineglass can be used to express how much wine there is, and vice versa.

Before we can go any further, we have to consider "**inversions**".

"**Inversion**" is the name that will be used, in this book, for a technique the Designer of the **Pi Encryption** has used, over and over again, to produce the wonderful designs and patterns that prove His handiwork in π.

According to the dictionary [(1)], an **inverse** ratio, or **inverse** proportion, exists "between two quantities such that one increases in proportion as the other decreases".

That seems to sum up perfectly the phenomenon we are considering.

For if a word (any word) can be expressed as a numerical quantity (see chapter 2), it can also be expressed as the **inversion** of that quantity.

To find a number's **inversion**, simply subtract it from an appropriate multiple of 1,000 above it.[(2)]

Thus the **inversion** of **386** ("Jesus" in Hebrew) can be **614** (using a field of 1,000 [(3)]), 1,**614** (using a field of 2,000), 2,**614** (using a field of 3,000), and so on.

Decimal fractions can also be **inverted** by subtracting them from 1[(4)].

You will become very familiar with **inversions** as we go on, so frequently have they been used in the composition of the **Pi Encryption**.

They occur so often, in fact, that one might be in danger of losing track of a very important fact -

that ALL inversions must inevitably be the product of a *mind* (5).

So whose *mind* was it, then, that built these into **Pi**?

Before we leave this chapter, let us consider two very simple examples of **inversions** that are found right near the surface of the **Pi Encryption**, yet lose none of their significance by virtue of being easily seen:

(1) **Key Point B** (6) (**3227186**) when **inverted** and halved, reveals **386** ("Jesus" in Hebrew):

- the **inversion** (in a field of 4,000,000): 4,000,000-3,227,186 = 772,814
- the halving: 772,814 ÷ 2 = **386**407 (7) "**JESUS**"

(2) The distance between **Key Points C** and **D** is 2,613,100, as follows:

	123,004,065	**Key Point D**
-	120,390,965	**Key Point C**
	2,613,100	

Now, 2,613,100 inverted in a field of 3,000,000 produces **386**900, as follows:

	3,000,000
-	2,613,100
	386,900 (7)

"JESUS"

Notes to chapter 8

(1) "The Oxford Dictionary of English", second Edition (revised), Oxford University Press, 2005.

(2) Or, if it is a decimal fraction, from 1.

(3) Ask any Jewish rabbi, and he will confirm that there are 613 commandments, or "Mitzvot" contained in the Torah. Jesus gave us one more, in John 13.34: "A new commandment I give unto you, that ye love one another; as I have loved you, that ye also love one another". Isn't it interesting that the addition of this one "new commandment" brings the total from 613 to 614 – which is the very inversion of Jesus' name?

(4) The inversion of 0.386 is 1-0.386 = 0.614.

(5) Like all mathematical operations, without exception.

(6) Here Key point B appears in its shortened form, i.e. after the subtraction from it of **Key Point A** (100,000,000) - see chapter 6, section 3.

(7) In the interests of avoiding any suspicion of exaggeration, these two examples of inversions will be grouped together, for the purposes of this book, as if they were only one - "Feature 3".

(8) **Hallmarks of Design in chapter 8.**

The presence of **386**, under the surface in these two examples, shows **consistency** and **purpose**, as well as conveying **information and meaning** (the name of "Jesus").

CHAPTER 8

CHAPTER 9

"JESUS IS GOD"

The meaning and importance of **614086**.

1. Introduction

This chapter is about **614,086**, an intriguing and highly significant component of the **Pi Encryption**.

The first point for us to note is that **614,086** seems to represent a combination of three deeply meaningful elements:

- **614**, (the **inversion** of **386**, "Jesus" in Hebrew)(1);
- a **zero**, indicating a break; and
- **86** (the numerical value of "God", in Hebrew)(2).

Without being in any way fanciful, **614086** can therefore be understood as a symbolic representation of the two separate and distinct words "Jesus" and "God" - effectively as a title, "Jesus God" - or, by extension, even as a statement that "Jesus is God".

And that clearly makes it of immense interest to us in this book.

2. How does 614,086 fit into the Pi Encryption?

It does so in at least three important ways (3), as set out below:

614086 – the first way

As we saw in chapter 6, the basic components of the **Pi Encryption** are the four **Key Points, A, B, C** and **D**, and the numbers of decimal places (or "distances") between them.

Now, the distance from **Key Point A** to **Key Point B** is **3,227,186** (4) decimal places, and that from **Key Point C** to **Key Point D** is **2,613,100** (5).

And the difference between these two distances is exactly **614,086** (6), as follows:

	3,227,186	
-	2,613,100	
	614,086	**"Jesus is God"**

614086 – the second way

As we saw in the Preface, the first section of the **Encryption Zone** ends at decimal place number 17,777,865 (counting from the beginning of the **Zone**).

It is also clear that the distance from **Key Point B** to **Key Point C** is 17,163,779 decimal places (7).

Now, the difference between these two highly significant numbers can be calculated very simply as follows:

	17,777,865	
-	17,163,779	
	614,086	**"Jesus is God"**

614086 – the third way

As we saw in chapter 6, **Key Position C** is to be found at decimal place number 20,390,965 (counting from the beginning of the **Encryption Zone**).

We have also seen that the distance from **Key Point B** to **Key Point D** is 19,776,879 decimal places (8).

Now, the difference between these two numbers is exactly **614,086**, as follows:

	20,390,965	
-	19,776,879	
	614,086	**"Jesus is God"**

3. Reflections on the "three ways"

At first glance, these three iterations of **614,086** may not seem particularly remarkable; but a moment's reflection should be sufficient to reveal, to every perceptive reader, how extremely unlikely it would be for such a mutually complementary network of results to arise by *chance*, rather than *design*.

Just think of how steeply the odds accumulate against such an orderly outcome, at each successive stage in the process:

Firstly — a number is *randomly* selected which *"just happens"* to be a complex palindrome (**17766771**) based on the name "Jesus" (see chapters 5 and 10);

Secondly — the first three occurrences of that number in **Pi** are identified – selecting **Key Points B**, **C** and **D** (*nota bene,* for all practical intents and purposes, this is yet another *random* selection, as no-one could ever predict or predetermine the outcome);

Thirdly — the other **Key Point** - **A** - is identified as being at the end of the first 100,000,000 decimal places in **Pi**;

Fourthly — the end of the First Section of the **Pi Encryption** (17,777,865) is also identified in the manner described in the Preface; and

Fifthly — all three of the distances shown in the first, second and third "ways" above are uncannily found to be exactly **614086** (signifying "**Jesus is God**").

4 – Author's aside

I would be the first to acknowledge that, if they stood alone, the numerical patterns described in this chapter might properly be dismissed, even by a highly intelligent person, as nothing more than a bizarre set of unusual coincidences. However, as they most definitely do not stand alone, they merit (indeed earnestly call for) every thinking reader's most careful consideration. You will notice, as you read on, how the gradual accumulation of mutually-corroborating data builds up into a compelling body of evidence. For this reason, as I have cautioned before, please be careful (for integrity's sake) to: (1) read this book to the very end; (2) until then, keep a truly open mind; and (3) reach your "verdict" without regard to any long-held personal preconceptions (however cherished they may be), but purely and simply on the basis of the *evidence* presented to you in this book.

Notes to chapter 9

(1) 1,000 - **386** = 614 (see chapter 8.)

(2) See Appendix 5.

(3) In accordance with this book's central policy of deliberately and massively *understating* the case for the **Pi Encryption**, all three of these "ways" in which **614068** appears in it will be bundled together as if they were only one – *"Feature 4"*.

(4) As **Key Points A** and **B** are at decimal place numbers 100,000,000 and 103,227,186 respectively, the distance between them is 3,227,186.

(5) As **Key Points C** and **D** are at decimal place numbers 120,390,965 and 123,004,065 respectively, the distance between them is 2,613,100.

(6) Given that **614086** is a 6 digit sequence, there is in fact no more than a million to one chance that it will appear randomly at any point. Even allowing for the fact that a number of alternative 6 digit combinations (such as the theoretically significant 386,086, 860,614 or 614,386) might have been regarded as equally significant had they been present, the chance of this (or a similar) potentially significant pattern existing at this point is still extremely remote - especially when one makes due allowance for the astronomically huge improbability of all the other key elements of the pattern (e.g. the triple involvement of **17766771**) also being present at the same time.

(7) As **Key Points B** and **C** are at decimal place numbers 103,227,186 and 120,390,965 respectively, the distance between them is 17,163,779.

(8) As **Key Points B** and **D** are decimal place numbers 103,227,186 and 123,004,065 respectively, the distance between them is 19,776,879.

A PAUSE TO REFLECT

"Information can only originate from an intelligent agent"

True or false?

If true, please identify the "intelligent agent" who has communicated to us the information "Jesus is God" by means of the three "ways" of feature 4.

CHAPTER 10

17766771 – THE MOST SUPERLATIVE PALINDROME - and the key to the Pi Encryption

A close look at the key to the **Pi Encryption**

I wrote earlier (1) that, on first encountering the number **17766771** (which is the key combination, or entrance code, to the **Pi Encryption**), I assumed it to be no more than a simple numerical palindrome based on twice **888** (2).

Later on, however, it became apparent that there really is a very great deal more to it than that - so much so that I can hardly believe it, even to this day!

The first four digits, 1,7,7 and 6, are clearly twice **888** ("Jesus" in Greek) - that much, at least, was plain from the start.

And for some time I thought that the last four digits, 6,7,7 and 1, were no more than the first four mirrored back, as one would expect in any ordinary palindrome.

But, in due course, an incredible truth dawned on me - that the last three figures (7,7 and 1), mirrored back by the first three (1,7 and 7),also mean "Jesus", only this time not expressed in Greek, but in Hebrew!

This is because, (just as half of 1776 is **<u>888</u>**, "Jesus" in Greek), half of 771 is 385.5, which is as close as the palindromic law (3) permits one to approach **<u>386</u>** ("Jesus" in Hebrew)!

The digit sequence **<u>17766771</u>** therefore is not only twice **<u>888</u>** *written both forwards and backwards*, but also represents twice **<u>386</u>** *written both backwards and forwards.*

It is a *double* (4), fully *reciprocating* (5) palindrome, formed out of two *doubled* (6) quantities, each with an *identical* (7) meaning ("Jesus"), yet expressed in a *different* Biblical language! (8)

What *perfect* symmetry! What an *absolute masterpiece* of design!

How many personal names, do you think, other than the wonderful name of "Jesus", would satisfy, so completely, such a rigorously demanding set of design constraints?

"A tiny few, if any" is the only possible answer!(9)

How amazing, then, to reflect that the name we are discussing here is no ordinary or common personal name, but that of the very One whom millions of people, all over the world, proclaim to be none other than:

<u>the Lord God Almighty - Creator of the Universe!</u>

Notes to chapter 10

(1) See chapter 5.

(2) As **888** is the numerical value of the letters of the name "Jesus" in Greek (see appendix 4), the quantity obtained by doubling it (1,776) will always be of great interest to any researcher in this field.

(3) "The palindromic law" is simply this, that anything that does not read exactly the same backwards as it does forwards, is not a palindrome. Twice **386** ("Jesus" in Hebrew) equals 772, which, if combined with 1776, would have resulted in the non-palindromic 17766772. It was necessary, therefore, in order for the palindromic law to be fully satisfied, for 772's next door neighbour, 771, to be used instead of 772, in order to form the perfect palindrome **17766771**, (which, as explained in this book, is a key combination code, the use of which is the only possible way to unlock the mysteries of the **Pi Encryption)**. It follows that **17766771** is not only the *near neighbour,* but, for the purposes of the Pi Encryption, truly the *alter ego*, of 17766772.

(4) *Double* in that two separate but overlapping elements, 1,776 and 771, are both palindromised. This will be referred to as "Feature 5".

(5) Fully *reciprocating* in that the two elements start on opposite sides and cross over, 1776 on the left answered by 6771 on the right, and 771 on the right answered by 177 on the left. This will be referred to as "Feature 6".

(6) *Doubled* in that 1,776 is twice **888** and 771 is as near to twice **386** as is possible without spoiling the palindrome. This will be referred to as "Feature 7".

(7) The *identical* meaning, of course, being "Jesus". This will be referred to as "Feature 8".

(8) The fact that *both* the Biblical languages (Hebrew and Greek) contribute equally to the formation of the key to the **Pi Encryption** is, of course, a powerful endorsement of both the Old and the New Testaments (written in Hebrew and Greek respectively) as integral parts of Holy Scripture.

(9) And, astonishingly, there is even more than this besides! For, as each occurrence in π of the key to the **Pi Encryption**, **17766771**, represents **8** iterations of the name of **JESUS**:

forwards:	1776	2 x 888	JESUS, JESUS
backwards:	6771	2 x 888	JESUS, JESUS
backwards:	177	2 x 386	JESUS, JESUS
forwards:	771	2 x 386	JESUS, JESUS
			8

and there are 3 such occurrences within the **Encryption Zone**, at **Key Points B**, **C** and **D**, then it follows that there are:

8,**8** and **8** (888) iterations of "Jesus" (**888** and **386**)

at the very foundation of the **Encryption Zone**!

Please ask yourself, honestly, whether such extraordinary marvels of design could possibly exist in the absence of a Designer.

However, in accordance with this book's core policy of always radically *understating* the case for the **Pi Encryption**, this pattern, wonderful though it is, will *not*, by being given its own Feature number, be included in chapter 28's probability calculation.

(10) **Hallmarks of Design in chapter 10.**

The significant grouping of 1776 with 6771 illustrates the use of a **system or process** (in the **symmetry** of a palindrome) to express **information and meaning** (the name of Jesus) with **accuracy, consistency** and in a way that evinces perfect **correspondence** between the Hebrew and Greek forms of the name "Jesus".

CHAPTER 11

"THE GOLDEN PATHWAY"

In this chapter, we discover *objective proof* of the reality of the **Pi Encryption**, in the form of pinpoint correspondences between *all four* of the **Key Points.**

1. Introduction

The "acid test" of whether the **Pi Encryption** truly exists as an *objective* reality (rather than merely as a *subjective* figment of this author's imagination), is whether its **Key Points** can be shown to bear relationships to each other which, rationally, could not have arisen except by the action of an external (and therefore an *objective*) agent.

In the same way, if a person merely *dreams* that his house has been burgled, one should not call the police unless evidence of an *actual* burglary (the work of an *external* agent) is found to exist.

In this chapter, we shall be taking a look at a prime example of just such a relationship, one that connects all of the **Key Points** to each other in an extraordinary yet undeniable pattern - a "golden pathway", running right through the **Encryption Zone**, from one end to the other, with incredible accuracy!

2. The Four Key Points

Firstly, let us remind ourselves what the four Key Points of the Encryption Zone are:

A.	**100,000,000**	the last decimal place in π before the **Zone**;
B.	**103,227,186**	the first,
C.	**120,390,965**	the second and
D.	**123,004,065**	the third occurrences, in **Pi**, of the digit-sequence **17766771**.

The significance of this "Golden Pathway", as you will see, is that it links all of these four **Key Points** to each other in an uncannily exact and intriguing way, which no truly impartial reader could ascribe to anything other than deliberate design.

3. The journey along "The Golden Pathway" – in six easy steps:

(1) **The First Step –**

is to start with **17766771** and identify its first three occurrences in Pi, which, as we saw above, are at decimal place numbers 103,227,186 (**Key Point B**), 120,390,965 (**Key Point C**) and 123,004,065 (**Key Point D**).

(2) **The Second Step –**

The second step on the "Golden Pathway" involves subtracting **Key Point A** from each of **Key Points C** and **D**, reducing them both by exactly 100,000,000, thus:

C. 120,390,965 - 100,000,000 = 20,390,965*
D. 123,004,065 - 100,000,000 = 23,004,065*

(* All further references to **Key Points C** and **D**, in this chapter, will be to their reduced forms of 20,309,965 and 23,004,065).

(3) **The Third Step**

Next, we take the last six digits of **Key Point B**, (2,2,7,1,8 and 6), and convert them into a decimal fraction, thus: 0.227186

(4) **The Fourth Step**

We then halve the last result, thus:
0.227186 ÷ 2 = 0.113593

(5) **The Fifth Step**

and **invert** it, thus: 1 - 0.113593 = 0.886407

(6) **The Sixth Step**

Finally, we take **Key Point D** (23,004,065) and multiply it by the result of the fifth step, 0.886407 – to arrive at the final result which,

amazingly ...

is none other than

Key Point C!

23,004,065 x 0.886407 = **20,390,965***

*(see notes 1 and 2)

4. "A moment's reflection"

A moment's reflection should be enough for anyone to appreciate not only the *objective* reality of this **"Golden Pathway"**, but also its breathtakingly profound significance.

Please take a moment to let this sink in.

Consider, for instance:

(1) **How Key Points A**, **B**, **C** and **D** are all exact and essential elements in this pattern - **D** having to be modified by the subtraction of **A**, before being combined with the last 6 digits of **B**, to produce the final result of **C**, which has also, like **D**, been modified by the subtraction of **A**!

(2) **How Key Points B**, **C** and **D**, by their intimate association with the key to the **Pi Encryption**, **17766771** (see chapter 10), clearly and unambiguously proclaim the name of **JESUS**;

(3) **How** *pinpoint precision* is present here, from beginning to end; and

(4) **How** *astronomically* improbable any of this would be, except by the hand of **Divine Providence**! (see notes 3, 4 and 5).

This "Golden Pathway" simply cannot be dismissed as anything other than the product of deliberate design!

Notes to chapter 11

(1) To the nearest whole decimal point above, and therefore "*with pinpoint precision*" (as that expression is defined in the Glossary).

(2) This will be referred to as "Feature 9".

(3) There are at least six essential elements (which are referred to in this note as elements "U" – "Z") in the composition of this "Golden Pathway", each and every one of which <u>must</u> be present, at the same time and place, for the Pathway not only to exist, but also to convey a significant meaning:

(i) there must be an eight-digit sequence ("U"), such as 17766771, which is capable (by reasonable interpretation, using conventional terms and criteria) of conveying a significant meaning, such as the name "Jesus" (see chapter 10);

(ii) there must be a number ("V"), such as 103227186, which is identified as being the decimal place number of the first occurrence of U in π;

(iii) a string of six digits ("W"), such as 227186, must form part of V, which, in a few easy steps (as shown in this chapter) can be used as a precise combination key-code to reveal the hidden Pathway;

(iv) there must be two further numbers ("X" and "Y"), such as 120390965 and 123004065, which, (like V), are also identified as being the decimal place numbers of occurrences of U in π, but this time the second and third ones; and

(v) there must be another number ("Z"), such as 100,000,000, which, when subtracted from both of X and Y, leaves remainders (such as 20390965 and 23004065) which are capable of being exactly linked to each other, *with pinpoint precision*, by the few easy steps shown in this chapter, using W as a key-code.

As removing or altering even one of these six essential elements would completely destroy the Pathway, the chance of its existing is exactly equal to that of all 6 of them occurring together at the same time and in their purest and most precise terms. Note (4) below contains an attempt to calculate the probability of elements W, X, Y and Z all occurring together, but (in accordance with this book's core policy of always massively *understating* the case for the Pi Encryption) elements U and V (although they are both of crucial importance in the formation of the Pathway) have been completely excluded from the calculation.

(4) **Element W.** The chance of any given sequence of six digits (such as 2,2,7,1,8 and 6) *if selected at random* being capable of linking up two other numbers (such as 23,004,065 and 20,390,965) by means of a "Golden Pathway" of this kind, in the manner described here, is arguably as low as one in a million (0.000001), as the randomly selected sequence could be anything from 000000 to 999999, providing a range of exactly 1,000,000 different sequences to select from. However, in order to avoid any suspicion of exaggeration, and in accordance with this book's core policy of always massively ***understating*** the case for the Pi Encryption, we shall (for the purpose of the present calculation)quite arbitrarily increase this chance a thousandfold, from one in a million (0.000001) to one in a thousand (0.001). **Elements X and Y**. The chance of both the relevant linked numbers happening to be identified (as in this case) as the decimal place-numbers of consecutive occurrences, in Pi, of a single eight digit sequence (such as 17766771) is one in a hundred million squared (1:100,000,000^2), as any given 8 digit sequence such as 17766771 can only reasonably be expected to occur, on average, once in every 100,000,000 digits of π (see chapter 5, note 2). **Elements W, X and Y combined**. It follows therefore that the combined probability of only those three of the six elements of "The Golden Pathway" which are referred to in note 3 above as elements "W", "X" and "Y", all being present together *randomly and by chance* (but not by design) can be no higher than one in one thousand x 100,000,000^2, or one chance in ten million trillion. **Element Z.** Yet even this is a massive understatement of the truly immense improbability with which we are faced here, as it gives no weight whatsoever to the double involvement of Key Point A, (element "Z") worth yet another 100,000,000^2 (or ten thousand trillion) to the count [because there is on average only one chance in 100,000,000 that any particular number between 1 and 100,000,000 will be selected by any random process for inclusion in a pattern of this kind. For exactly the same number to be selected twice, as occurs here, the chance of success, if the selection is random, is only 1:100,000,000^2 (one chance in ten thousand trillion)]. **Elements W, X, Y and Z combined**. The overall likelihood, therefore, of all these four separate but essential elements (elements W-Z described in note 3 above) of a *complex, elaborate and exact* pattern such as the "Golden Pathway" occurring at the same time, in the same place, but by accident and not by design, can certainly be no higher than one chance in 10^{35}, that is, **one chance in one hundred billion, trillion, trillion.**

To get a grasp on just how huge this number is, the following illustration may help:

as the journey from Earth to Alpha Centauri (the nearest star to our solar system) is about 25 trillion miles, you would have to travel there and back about two billion trillion times, in order to clock up a similar number of miles – equivalent to over 4,500 round trips between Earth and Alpha Centauri every second since (according to proponents of the "Big Bang Theory") the Universe began 13.8 billion years ago!

But, as stated in note 3 above, even this huge number takes no account at all of the meaning of **17766771** ("Jesus" – see chapter 10), or of its structured, ordered and obviously designed characteristics ("U"), or of the fact that decimal place number 103227186 ("V") marks its first appearance in Pi. In brief, the *real* odds *against* a random origin for "The Golden Pathway", from beginning to end, and taking full account of all its many complex elements, are *incalculably* high.

(5) One may fairly ask just how and why the "Golden Pathway" works out as accurately as it does. The best answer I can offer is that, by Divine Providence, the last six digits of Key Point B (2,2,7,1,8 and 6), are precisely calibrated, by combination with Key Point D (23,004,065), to demarcate the combined Second and Third Sections of the Encryption Zone (please refer to the Preface), thus:

> 23,004,065 x 0.227186 = 5,226,201.5 (or twice 2,613,100.75, the length of each of the Second and Third Sections of the Encryption Zone being 2,613,100).

Now, it follows that if 0.227186 is halved and inverted (as shown in the third and fourth steps above in this chapter) and then multiplied by the overall length of the **Zone** (Key Point D minus Key Point A) it will *exactly* produce the upper limit of the Second Section, known in this book as Key Point C, thus:

> 23,004,065 x 0.886407 = 20,390,965 (to the nearest decimal place above it)

The most important phrase in the above, however, to which I make no apology for returning, is "by Divine Providence", as, in this author's opinion, no other explanation can rationally be offered for any of the contents of this chapter.

(6) **Hallmarks of Design in chapter 11**.

We see a definite **system or process** in the six steps of the "Golden Pathway", each resulting in an **orderly** fashion from what came before, and proceeding in an **orderly** fashion through to its conclusion.

We also see quite astonishing pinpoint **accuracy** in the way that the **orderly** combination of **Key Points A**, **B** and **D** exactly produce **Key Point C**, and **information and meaning** is implicit in this seamless interweaving of the first three instances of the key to the **Pi Encryption** - **17766771** ("Jesus"). We also see an overarching **consistency**, both of technique and message, between this and all the other features of the **Pi Encryption** which are presented before and after it in this book.

CHAPTER 12

STRANGELY LINKED

How the first three occurrences, in π, of the Key to the **Pi Encryption**, **(17766771)** are strangely linked to each other.

At first glance, the first three appearances in Pi of the key to the **Pi Encryption**, **17766771,** do not seem to have very much in common with each other.

Let us remind ourselves what they are:

The first (which we are calling **Key Point B**) begins at decimal place number:	**1032**27186
The second (Key Point C) begins at decimal place number:	**1203**90965
The third (Key Point D) begins at decimal place number:	**1230**04065

Now let us look a little more closely at these three key numbers. When we do, we see that they all share a very interesting characteristic - that their first four digits are all 0, 1, 2 or 3:

Key Point B: **1032**
Key Point C: **1203**
Key Point D: **1230**

Now this may not seem, on the face of it, to be anything very remarkable – until, that is, one realizes that the chance of such a pattern arising "accidentally", i.e. by pure chance, is very small indeed – considerably smaller, in fact, than one's chance of flipping a coin 26 times in a row with the same result (26 consecutive "heads" or 26 consecutive "tails") each and every time [(1)].

The actual likelihood of this phenomenon occurring randomly is only one chance in 125,000,000, a probability of 0.000000008! [(2)].

In other words, if the selection process is conducted at random, by pure chance, one can only reasonably expect to select a similar combination of digits, on average, once in every 125,000,000 attempts!

We see then, that **Key Points B**, **C** and **D** are *strangely linked* [(3)], not only by being the first three occurrences in Pi of the digit sequence **17766771**, but also by defying all the odds and having their first 4 digits in common - a combined probability of 1:(125,000,000 x 10^{24}), or **one chance in one hundred and twenty-five million trillion trillion!** [(4)] [(5)].

Can we not agree (leaving all prejudices aside) that such an extraordinarily unlikely pattern, if it were given in testimony at a trial, would be accepted, by any fair-minded jury, as overwhelming evidence of the existence of a *design* (and therefore, by necessary implication, of a *designer)?*

Or, if a suspect's DNA matched that of the offender to such an incredible degree, his conviction (in the absence of a rock-solid alibi, proving that he was actually somewhere else when the crime was committed) would be virtually inevitable?

Notes to chapter 12

(1) 0.5^{26} = 0.00000001490, or one chance in 67,114,094 - which is the probability of an unbroken chain of 26 heads or 26 tails resulting from 26 consecutive flips of a coin. Thus the chance of tossing a coin 26 times with the result being 26 heads (and no tails) or 26 tails (and no heads) is nearly twice as great as that of three randomly-selected four-digit numbers all containing the same digits, as we have observed in this chapter (which is one chance in 125,000,000).

(2) See Appendix 6 for the relevant calculations.

(3) This pattern will be referred to as "Feature 10".

(4) This huge figure is calculated as follows: (a) the probability of any three numbers, *if selected at random and without deliberate design*, happening to represent consecutive place numbers in π of the same 8 digit sequence (such as **17766771**) is $1:100,000,000^3$ (see chapter 5, note 2); (b) the probability of any three numbers, *if selected at random and without deliberate design* all sharing the same first four digits is 1:125,000,000 (see Appendix 6); (c) the combined probability therefore of any three numbers (such as **Key Points B**, **C** and **D**) *if selected at random and without deliberate design* all sharing both the attributes mentioned in (a) and (b) above, is 125,000,000 x 10^{24}, or one chance in 125 million trillion trillion.

(5) The depth and complexity of this pattern are further enhanced by two additional elements: (1) the four digits that feature in it (0, 1, 2 and 3), represent a linear progression from zero (representing the beginning of π) through the 1st and 2nd occurrences in Pi of **17766771**, to the 3rd occurrence, covering the whole section of π in which the **Pi Encryption** is found; and (2) furthermore, by the placing of the 3 zeros, the first occurrence in π of **17766771** is demarcated as "1", the second as "1,2" and the third as "1,2,3". The digits could so easily have been any other combination - such as 3, 6, 7 and 9, or 2, 4, 5 and 8 - which could have borne no such meanings. If they were included in the calculation (which I shall refrain from doing, in order to avoid any charge of exaggeration) these extraordinary *additional* elements would most certainly increase the already enormous odds (against *randomness* and in favour of *design*), by a very substantial factor.

(6) **Hallmarks of Design in chapter 12.**

The **significant grouping** of the first three occurrences in Pi of the key to the **Pi Encryption** (**17766771** - "Jesus" x 8 – see chapter 10, note 9) in such positions that the first four digits of the decimal place number of each of them shows such pronounced **correspondence** with the other two, is replete with **information and meaning** ("Jesus") which is wholly **consistent** with the **message** and **methodology** evident throughout the **Pi Encryption**.

CHAPTER 13

"TIMES FOUR" - TWO STEPS TO GLORY!

A very simple and direct example of God's perfect design in the Pi Encryption.

Introduction

We have seen previously (in chapter 7) how, in any research of this kind, patterns based on **386** and **888** are of particular interest.

This is because both these numbers represent the name of Jesus, **386** in Hebrew and **888** in Greek.

Both of them are integral parts of **17766771**, the key to the **Pi Encryption** (see chapter 10) and they both recur time and time again as essential components of the interlocking patterns at the heart of the **Encryption**.

In this chapter, we shall look briefly at yet another very simple example of how these two wonderful numbers have been seamlessly integrated into the core structure of the **Pi Encryption**, as a sign to the world of the identity of its Creator - a maker's mark, or signature, in witness of His handiwork.

First Step

If we take the decimal place numbers of the first three occurrences, in Pi, of the key to the **Pi Encryption**, 17766771, (Key Points B, C and D) and add them together, we obtain 346,622,216:

103,227,186	**Key Point B**
120,390,965	**Key Point C**
+ 123,004,065	**Key Point D**
346,622,216	

"Nothing special there", you may say - but:

Second Step

Simply multiply that result by 4[(1)], and we come immediately into the presence of the Divine Glory[(2)(3)(4)]:

346,622,216 x 4 =

1,	**386**	4	**888**	64
	"JESUS" (in Hebrew)		**"JESUS"** (in Greek)	

<u>Author's Comment</u>

I did not create this pattern by trickery or falsehood. That would have been impossible for me to do, even if I had wanted to! The simple fact is that it exists – and has existed since the beginning of time, (or rather since the beginning of π, whichever came first!) Taken simply by itself, I readily admit that it does not prove anything at all. But, taken together with all the other patterns described in this book, it contributes significantly to an extremely compelling case for Design. Please keep reading, because a convincing body of even stronger, and mutually corroborating, evidence lies ahead.

Notes to chapter 13

(1) 4 is one of the few accepted "step factors" (see Glossary).

(2) This will be referred to as "Feature 11".

(3) Compare this with chapter 17, in which the sum of all 4 Key Points (and not just 3 of them as in this chapter), when exposed to a similarly simple mathematical process, produces an equally remarkable result.

(4) The probability of both **386** and **888** (or any other pair of three digit numbers) appearing together in a *randomly generated* sequence of 8 digits (such as 38614888, 88841386, etc) is only one chance in over 83,000 (1:83,333.33'), calculated as follows:

   (i) for any given pair of three-digit sequences (such as **386** and **888**), there are only 1,200 eight-digit sequences within which they can both be found together (as in 13864888, 38614888, 88838614, etc);

   (ii) there is a total of 100,000,000 eight digit sequences, from 00000000 to 99999999 inclusive;

   (iii) the chance of any *randomly selected* 8 digit sequence containing both a **386** and an **888** is therefore one chance in (100,000,000 divided by 1,200), or 1:83,333.

(N.B. this tiny probability – considerably less than one's chance of tossing 17 heads (or 17 tails) in 17 successive tosses of a coin - still takes no account at all of the important fact that **386** and **888** are the numerical values of the name "Jesus" in Hebrew and Greek. Were this extra element somehow to be factored in, the probability of such a result would be much smaller still; but tipping the balance the other way, is the fact that other combinations (such as 614 and 888, two 888's, two 386's etc) would, if found here, have been considered equally remarkable, thus increasing the probability of a significant outcome. Whilst a definitive estimate of probability can never be confidently propounded, the fact remains that Feature 11 represents an astonishingly direct and undeniable numerical "bridge" between 17766771 (represented by its first three appearances in Pi) and those two great numbers (386 and 888) of which it is composed (see chapter 10).

(5) **Hallmarks of Design in chapter 13**

In the selection of our raw material at the beginning of the process (the first three occurrences in Pi of the digit-string **17766771** - "Jesus") there is **order**, **significant grouping**, **consistency** and **information and**

meaning. In adding them together and multiplying the result by four, there is the application of a **system or process** which is **consistent** with others presented in this book (e.g. features 15 and 16 in chapters 17 and 18). The result, 1,3864 88864, **accurately** conveys **information and meaning** (the name of Jesus in two Biblical languages) which is entirely **consistent** with the raw material (**17766771** - "Jesus") we started with. Finally, and perhaps most amazingly, we see **correspondence** between the digits of Pi (in the form of **17766771** - "Jesus") and their decimal place numbers in Pi (in the form of **Key Points B**, **C** and **D**), although of course the two should (by conventional reasoning) be entirely independent of each other. (For another, even more striking, example of this, please see chapter 20).

CHAPTER 13

CHAPTER 14

"MAGNIFYING JESUS"

This chapter describes how the length of the **Encryption Zone** expresses, with *incredible accuracy*, the ratio between the numerical values of the name "Jesus" in Hebrew and Greek.

1. Introduction

I have no doubt that, to many, the **Pi Encryption** will seem so strange, even alien, that despite all the supporting material, they will reject it outright.

Such people may, even against their own inner convictions, deny the true strength of the evidence, for fear of accepting it and, in consequence, having to reconsider their most cherished preconceptions.

However, in order to maintain such an uncomfortable position with any shred of credibility, they will need to come up with alternative explanations for the "inconvenient truths" presented in this book: explanations which at least *appear* to be both reasonable and evidence-based.

It will indeed be very interesting to see how they account for the (to them) disconcerting fact that **386** ("Jesus" in Hebrew), when multiplied by the length of the **Encryption Zone**, increases to *exactly* **888** ("Jesus" in Greek).

Yes, it really does!

It is as if the name "Jesus" in Hebrew (**<u>386</u>**), when "magnified" through a "lens" equivalent in strength to the length of the **<u>Encryption Zone</u>**, is transformed into none other than **<u>888</u>** ("Jesus" in Greek).

As one of the meanings of the verb "to magnify" is "to praise highly, glorify" (1) (as in "Praise the Lord and magnify Him"), it seems appropriate to name this chapter "Magnifying Jesus".

<u>2. The Jesus Magnification</u>

The **Jesus Magnification** is the rock-solid and mathematically robust link that undoubtedly exists between **<u>386</u>** ("Jesus" in Hebrew), **<u>23,004,065</u>** (the length of the **<u>Encryption Zone</u>**) (2) and **<u>888</u>** ("Jesus" in Greek).

In order to keep the numbers we have to deal with reasonably manageable, we will start by reducing **<u>23,004,065</u>** to **<u>2.3004065</u>** (3).

This does not in any way affect the validity of the results, but it does cut down the number of zeros we have to use in order to express them!

- If you take **<u>386</u>** and magnify/multiply it by **<u>2.3004065</u>**, the result is **<u>888</u>** (4).
- And if you take **<u>888</u>** and reduce/divide it by **<u>2.3004065</u>**, the result is **<u>386</u>** (4).

THE LENGTH OF THE ENCRYPTION ZONE (<u>23,004,065</u>) REPRESENTS, *WITH PINPOINT ACCURACY*, THE RATIO BETWEEN THE NAME OF <u>JESUS</u> (386) WHEN EXPRESSED IN HEBREW, AND THE NAME OF <u>JESUS</u> (888) WHEN EXPRESSED IN GREEK! (5)

<u>3. Conclusion</u>

There are two main dangers facing us at this point:

- the **first** is to imagine that this is something small, trivial and inconsequential - yet how could it be, when **Pi** is at the very foundation of the whole created order?
- The **second** is to imagine that these facts are without meaning - yet the encryption of God's very name in Pi - the fundamental constant of His creation - could scarcely be more significant.

Do we not owe it to ourselves to reflect carefully for a moment, if we are not to risk missing what may be the most important message we will ever hear?

This fundamental pattern in the **Pi Encryption** is nothing less than an exquisitely crafted masterpiece of design, and an abiding proof, not only of the genius of its Divine Designer, but also of His love for all mankind in **JESUS OUR LORD**.

The Jesus Magnification was deliberately and purposely designed, and has now truly been revealed *for our good*, to glorify that mighty name and to draw souls into His Kingdom.

Please do not leave this chapter until you have re-read and dwelt on it for as long as is necessary to obtain full realisation of this wonderful truth.

Notes to chapter 14

(1) Oxford Dictionary of English, Second edition, revised, Oxford University Press, 2006.

(2) The length of the **Encryption Zone** is the number of decimal places in π from **Key Point A** (100,000,000) to **Key Point D** (123,004,065), that is to say:

$$\begin{array}{r} 123{,}004{,}065 \\ -\ \underline{100{,}000{,}000} \\ 23{,}004{,}065 \end{array}$$

For more on the 4 **Key Points** please turn to chapter 6.

(3) **23,004,065** divided by 10,000,000 = **2.3004065**. Doing this saves us having to deal with 8,880,000,000 instead of 888, but apart from this the process and the results are both identical.

(4) If you check these figures on a calculator, you will find that the exact results are 887.956909 and 386.018732, which differ from 888 and 386 by only one part in 20,607 (less than 5 in 100,000) - a very high degree of accuracy, and more than sufficient, for present purposes, to justify my use of the word “exactly” in the text. To illustrate this, imagine yourself in a 100,000 seat sports stadium, packed to capacity with fans. Now, if 5 of the 100,000 fans are discreetly removed from various parts of the stadium, is the stadium any less full? Would anyone even notice the 5 missing fans’ absence? That is how *incredibly accurate* this **Jesus Magnification** really is!

Yet, for those who may still insist on quibbling, even this tiny remainder (almost too small to merit our attention), itself resolves, by inversion, into 888 thus:

$$10{,}000 - \left(\left[\left(\frac{888}{386}\right) \mathrm{x} \left(\frac{A}{10}\right)\right] - 23{,}004{,}065\right) = \underline{888}_{3.65}$$

(5) As we have already mentioned this, in much less detail, in chapter 7, where it was included as one of the 6 elements of “Feature 2”, no new feature number will be assigned to it here.

(6) **Hallmarks of Design in chapter 14.**

We see with what incredible **accuracy** (true to 5 parts in 100,000) this pattern conveys **information and meaning** (the name of Jesus in two Biblical languages - 386 and 888), exhibiting specific **correspondence** (through that same wonderful name) with the key to the **Encryption Zone** - 17766771 (Jesus 386 and Jesus 888 - see chapter 10). We also see with what **consistency** this reflects the whole theme of the **Pi Encryption** (to *magnify* the name of Jesus) and how a **system or process** (the establishment of the ratio between **386** and **888**) has been instrumental in determining the placing of **Key Point D** (the third occurrence of **17766771** - Jesus) at that precise point in Pi (exactly **2300465** decimal places after **Key Point A**) which it has occupied since before time began.

CHAPTER 15

A LITTLE "FOOLISHNESS"

How the three distances between **Key Points B**, **C** and **D** combine together to glorify the name of **JESUS**.

There are only three distances separating **Key Points B**, **C** and **D**, (which, as we already know, share the distinction of being the first three occurrences, in π, of the digit-string **17766771**).

They are:

From **B** to **C**(1)	17,163,779	decimal places;
From **B** to **D**(2)	19,776,879	decimal places; and
From **C** to **D**(3)	2,613,100	decimal places.

As **17766771** derives its significance from the name of Jesus (**888** and **386** – see chapter 10), a person who believed in the **Pi Encryption** would not find it at all strange if those three distances, when combined together mathematically in a simple way, produced the number **888** – in fact, he might even expect them to!

Yet, to someone who did not believe in the **Pi Encryption**, such an expectation would be *foolish in the extreme.*

Well, St. Paul the apostle once wrote that the foolishness of God is wiser than men(4).

Before we can put this to the test to see who is right, we first need to reduce each of the three distances by a factor of one million[(5)], so that:

17,163,779	becomes	17.163779;
19,776,879	becomes	19.776879; and
2,613,100	becomes	2.6131

Now, simply multiply the three distances together, and the result is as near to **888** as makes no difference![(6)] [(7)]

And so we can clearly see that we should never be afraid of looking "foolish" for the sake of Christ.

<u>Notes to chapter 15</u>

(1) As **Key Point B** is at decimal place number 103,227,186 and **Key Point C** is at place number 120,390,965, the distance from B to C is 17,163,779 decimal places, thus:

C	120,390,965
B	- 103,227,186
	17,163,779

(2) As **Key Point B** is at decimal place number 103,227,186 and **Key Point D** is at decimal place number 123,004,065, the distance from B to D is 19,776,879 decimal places, thus:

D	123,004,065
B	- 103,227,186
	19,776,879

(3) As **Key Point C** is at decimal place number 120,390,965 and **Key Point D** is at decimal place number 123,004,065, the distance from C to D is 2,613,100 decimal places, thus:

D	123,004,065
C	- 120,390,965
	2,613,100

(4) 1 Corinthians 1, verse 25.

(5) This is for presentation purposes only, and makes no substantive difference at all to the pattern we are discussing.

(6) The exact result is actually 887.006291555, so close to 888 that the pattern is both striking and unmistakeable. However, as there will always be some who will quibble, I cannot refrain from pointing out that even the tiny shortfall we see here itself resolves neatly, against high odds, into <u>**888**</u>, thus:

$$\frac{887.006291555}{888} = 0.99\ \underline{\mathbf{888}}\ 095$$

The probability of such a sequence arising randomly can be reliably calculated at only one chance in 333.33, as follows:

a) the sequence 99888 is one of the 100,000 five-digit sequences from 00000 to 99999 inclusive;
b) only 300 of the said 100,000 five digit sequences contain the sequence <u>888</u>;
c) therefore the probability that 888 will feature in any *randomly generated* 5 digit sequence is 300:100,000 or 1:333.33.

(7) This will be referred to as “Feature 12”.

CHAPTER 15

CHAPTER 16

THREE TRUTHFUL WITNESSES

How **KEY POINTS B**, **C** and **D** combine with each other, in pairs, to give us the name of **JESUS** in *both* the Biblical languages.

Introduction

Studying the **Pi Encryption** is a bit like a treasure hunt, in which there is an unlimited store of treasure to be found, if only one keeps on looking! Or like a gold rush, where it's the gold that comes rushing to the prospector, and not the other way round! In this chapter, we shall be looking at three very simple combinations, all with telling results – results which, especially when taken together with all the other evidence presented in this book, make it even more ridiculous to deny the existence of a deep underlying plan. **Our quest** is to find occurrences of **386** ("**Jesus**" in Hebrew) and **888** ("**Jesus**" in Greek) which arise from simple mathematical combinations of **Key Points** of the **Encryption Zone**. The combinations can be by addition, subtraction, multiplication, or division, so long as they all exhibit that recurrent characteristic of the **Pi Encryption** – *childish simplicity*.

As we have seen, there are three **Key Points** that represent the first three iterations, in π, of the digit-string **17766771** – **B, C and D.**

It follows that there are only three ways in which they can be combined with each other in groups of two:

B with **D** "the First Witness"

B with **C** "the Second Witness"

C with **D** "the Third Witness"

Now let's examine these in turn:

1. The First Truthful Witness
Key Points B and D – 386 in three moves

As we have already noted many times, **Key Points B** and **D** mark the first and third occurrences, in π, of the digit-string **17766771**, the Key to the **Pi Encryption**. They are:

Key Point B	103,227,186
Key Point D	123,004,065

First move - addition

The first move is simply to add them together:

$$\begin{array}{r} 103{,}227{,}186 \\ +123{,}004{,}065 \\ \hline 226{,}231{,}251 \end{array}$$

Second move - subtraction

Next, we invert the result:

$$\begin{array}{r} 1{,}000{,}000{,}000 \\ -\ \ 226{,}231{,}251 \\ \hline 773{,}768{,}749 \end{array}$$

Third move - division

And finally, we halve it:

773,768,749 ÷ 2 = **386**$_{884374.5}$ **"JESUS"** (1)

2. The Second Truthful Witness
Key Points B and C – 888 in three moves

As we already know, **Key Points B** and **C** are the first and second occurrences, in π, of **17766771**:

Key Point B	103,227,186
Key Point C	120,390,965

First move - addition

As in section 1 ("the First Witness"), the first move is simply to add them together:

$$\begin{array}{r} 103{,}227{,}186 \\ +\underline{120{,}390{,}965} \\ 223{,}618{,}151 \end{array}$$

Second move - division

Next, we halve it:

$$223{,}618{,}151 \div 2 = 111{,}809{,}075.5$$

Third move - subtraction

And finally, we invert it:

$$\begin{array}{r} 1{,}000{,}000{,}000.00 \\ -\quad 111{,}809{,}075.50 \\ \hline \end{array}$$

888190,924.50 **"JESUS"** (2)

Author's aside

You may already have noticed how very similar the three moves are in each of the first two "witness" combinations – they both start with an addition, followed (in the first "witness") by an inversion and then a halving, and (in the second "witness") a halving and then an inversion. The only difference between them is in the order of the second and third moves. Such striking similarities make the first two combinations (which, by worldly wisdom, should have no similarity whatsoever) into high-grade, mutually-corroborating witnesses of their own common **DESIGN**.

As always, it is for each reader to decide independently on the identity of the **DESIGNER**.

But, for me, there is only one possible answer – and **386** ("Jesus") and **888** ("Jesus") are both rather obvious clues!

But wait, we have yet to study the third "truthful witness"!

3. The Third Truthful Witness
Key Points C and D – 386 in two moves

If (as we have seen above) simple combinations of **Key Points B** with **D** and **B** with **C** both produce numerical expressions of the name of Jesus, would it not seem strange (assuming the **Pi Encryption** to be real) if a similar result could not also be obtained from combining **Key Points C** and **D**?

Indeed, could not the *absence* of such a feature be used as an argument *against* the existence of the **Encryption**?

Well, fear not – God's Providence never fails! Though it follows a slightly different (but even simpler) path from that of the first two, the third truthful witness is present nonetheless, as clear and as unmistakeable as its two earlier companions.

And here it is:

First move - subtraction

The first move is simply to subtract **Key Point C** from **Key Point D**, thus:

D	123,004,065
C	- 120,390,965
	2,613,100

Second Move – also subtraction

Next, we invert the result, thus:

3,000,000
- 2,613,100
386,900 **"JESUS"** (3)

How could three such truthful witnesses, all agreeing with each other and incapable of lying or being changed, be guilty of giving false testimony?

A challenge from the author

I challenge any reader to produce another example of three 9 digit numbers, such as **Key Points B, C** and **D,** which are capable, in the manner described above, of producing equivalent results. They must, when paired off with each other in three groups of two, and subjected to three simple two or three stage *mathematical processes* such as we have seen, all produce one of a given pair of numbers (such as **386** and **888**), that are both numerically linked, in Hebrew or Greek, to a single person's name (such as "Jesus"), as shown in this chapter. If anyone can achieve such a herculean feat, he is already deserving of great honour and praise. But, in order to win the victor's crown, he must then go two, immensely difficult, further steps on:

(1) firstly, he must demonstrate that the three 9 digit numbers he is offering for our consideration are all related to each other, (through π and a common eight digit key combination, such as 17766771), in a similar way to that in which these three, **Key Points B, C** and **D**, are undoubtedly related. In other words, they must all represent decimal place numbers in π that are the first, second and third occurrences of the same eight digit number sequence. As any person of good sense and sound judgment will readily acknowledge, such a task will be impossible to discharge, even *without* the final, yet equally essential, requirement (if this book's theory of design is to be falsified), namely that:

(2) the reader's eight digit key combination must be a *perfect palindrome*(4) (such as 17766771) formed from the *very same* pair of numbers (such as **386** and **888**) that were produced by the three *mathematical processes* mentioned above. In other words, the given pair of numbers (such as **386** and **888**) must form both the *beginning* of the process, and, after passing through the complex medium of π, its *ultimate conclusion.*

Is there anyone at all who cannot plainly see, in light of all this, how absolutely *preposterous* it is to deny the existence, in these deep and wonderful **patterns**, of the clearest possible

EVIDENCE OF DESIGN?

Notes on chapter 16

(1) This will be referred to as "Feature 13"

(2) This will be referred to as "Feature 14".

(3) As this has already been referred to in chapter 8 as one of the two components of Feature 3, no separate feature number will be given to it here.

(4) See chapter 10.

CHAPTER 16

CHAPTER 17

THREE SIMPLE STEPS

Here we see how the sum of the four **Key Points**, when halved and inverted, speaks clearly of **JESUS**.

What would it take to convince you that there is a *clear and unmistakable* connection between the four **Key Points** and the name of Jesus?

On the face of it, they are just "ordinary" numbers - long ones admittedly, but "ordinary" nonetheless:

Key Point A	100,000,000
Key Point B	103,227,186
Key Point C	120,390,965
Key Point D	123,004,065

There is nothing, just from looking at them, even remotely to suggest that the wonderful name of **JESUS** is embedded within them, just three easy steps from the surface, and accessible to everyone by a simple process of decryption.

Before showing you how this works, I would ask you to reflect for a moment on how astronomically *unlikely* it would be for four nine-digit numbers like these, *if they were chosen at random*, to be capable of producing, *in three simple steps*, a ten-digit sequence which includes both **1776** (twice **888** = "Jesus, Jesus") and **888** ("Jesus").

Yet, even against those *astronomically high* odds, that is *precisely* what these do [(1)]!

And here is how it works:

(1) **First Step - addition**

Add the four **Key Points** together –

	100,000,000	(A)
	103,227,186	(B)
	120,390,965	(C)
+	123,004,065	(D)
	446,622,216	

(2) **Second Step - division**

Now, divide the result of the first step by 2 (see note 2):

$$446{,}622{,}216 \div 2 = 223{,}311{,}108$$

(3) **Third and final Step - subtraction**

Finally, **invert** the last result, by subtracting it from 2,000,000,000, producing:

	2,000,000,000
-	223,311,108
=	**1776**6**888**92

"JESUS, JESUS, JESUS" (3) (4)

Author's remarks

It is an amazing fact that a tiny difference of just 16 decimal places (for instance, if **Key Point B** had been at place number 103,227,170 instead of 103,227,186) would have been enough to annihilate this result, giving us **1776**6889OO instead of **1776**6**888**92.

Such a microscopically tiny margin of error (the equivalent of just one decimal place in over 27,900,000) shouts out one thing, and one thing only- "**DELIBERATE DESIGN!**"

Can't you hear it?

Or is it just that you don't *want* to hear it?

Please search your heart for the true answer, *and don't believe any lies* - **this whole subject is simply far too important for anything but complete, determined and relentless honesty**.

Notes on chapter 17:

(1) This will be referred to as "Feature 15". Interestingly, exactly the same digit sequence, **1776**$_{6}$**888**$_{92}$, is arrived at, but by a completely different route, in Feature 26 (see chapter 22).

(2) 2 is one of the small number of "step factors" which are accepted, in this book, for use when computing the Pi Encryption (see the Glossary for more on this).

(3) Compare this with chapter 13, in which the sum of Key Points B, C and D, when exposed to a similarly simple mathematical process, produces an equally remarkable result.

(4) The probability of both **1776** and **888** (or any other combination of a four and a three digit number) appearing together in a *randomly selected* sequence of 8 digits (such as 17766888, 88861776, etc) is only one chance in one million six hundred and sixty-six thousand (1:1,666,666), calculated as follows:

- (i) there are only 60 eight-digit sequences (such as 17766888, 88861776, etc) within which **1776** and **888** can both be found together;
- (ii) there is a total of 100,000,000 eight-digit sequences, from 00000000 to 99999999 inclusive;
- (iii) the chance that any *randomly selected* eight-digit sequence will contain both a 1776 and an 888 is therefore one chance in 100,000,000 divided by 60, or 1:1,666,666.

(N.B. This tiny probability – considerably less than one's chance of tossing 20 heads (or 20 tails) in 20 successive tosses of a coin, still takes no account at all of the important fact that both **1776** and **888** signify the name "Jesus", as 888 is the numerical value of that name in Greek, and 1776 is twice 888. Were this extra element somehow to be factored in, the probability of such a result would be much smaller still; but, tipping the balance the other way, is the fact that other combinations (such as 1776 and 386, 1776 and 614, etc) would, if found here, have been considered equally remarkable, thus increasing the probability of a significant outcome. Whilst a definitive estimate of probability can never be confidently propounded, the fact remains that Feature 15 represents an astonishing, and undeniable, numerical "bridge" between the four Key Points and the name of Jesus in Greek).

(5) **Hallmarks of Design in chapter 17**.

Here we see **order**, **significant grouping**, **consistency** and **information and meaning** in the selection of the four **Key Points** with which this calculation begins, and the application of an **orderly system or process** to arrive at the result, **consistent** both in methodology and outcome with features 11 (see chapter 13) and 16 (see chapter 18), as well as with the overall theme and inspiration of the **Pi Encryption** (the name of Jesus). We also see striking **correspondence** between the digits of Pi (in the form of **17766771** - "Jesus" - which underlies **Key Points B**, **C** and **D**) and the outworking of the sum (**1776** and **888** - "Jesus", "Jesus") although the two should, were no design present, be entirely independent of each other.

CHAPTER 17

CHAPTER 18

JESUS, FROM JESUS, THROUGH JESUS

Here we see how **Key Points B**, **C** and **D** are not only the first three occurrences in Pi of **17766771** ("Jesus"), but also, in close combination with **Key Point A**, carry it embedded within them.

In the last chapter, we saw how easy it is to use the four **Key Points** to calculate a ten-digit number which includes both **1776** and **888**, by a simple three step process involving addition, division and subtraction.

But **1776** and **888**, crucial though they are to the whole fabric of the **Pi Encryption**, are not themselves the unique and indispensable "key" that is an essential requirement in order to gain access to it.

There is only one such key, and that is undoubtedly the digit sequence **17766771** (see chapter 10).

If anyone were to ask whether it is possible, by a similarly short and simple process applied to the four **Key Points**, to *exactly* reproduce that precious key **17766771**, I would have to answer no - not as far as I know.(1)

Or at least, not *quite*!

Not *absolutely and completely!*

But it *is* possible to produce, in four simple steps, a number that, as it contains both of its significant components - **1776** and **771** – is so close to 17766771 that the evidence of deliberate design is unmistakable (2).

And this is how it works (3):

Step One - addition

Add up the decimal place numbers of the first three occurrences, in **Pi**, of the key to the **Pi Encryption** 17766771 -

Key Point B	103,227,186
Key Point C	120,390,965
Key Point D	123,004,065
	346,622,216

Step Two - multiplication

Multiply the result of Step One by a decimal fraction made up of the last eight digits of **Key Point B** (4). As **Key Point B** is 103,227,186, its last eight digits are 0,3,2,2,7,1,8 and 6, thus:

346,622,216 x 0.**03227186** = 11,186,143.628

Step Three - subtraction

Next, invert the result of Step Two by subtracting it from **Key Point A** (100,000,000), thus:

	100,000,000.000
-	11,186,143.628
	88,813,856.372

Fourth and Final Step - multiplication

And finally, double the result of Step Three, to arrive at:

88,813,856.372 x 2 = **1776** 2 **771** 2.

"JESUS, JESUS"

A long hard look

Let's stand back for a moment and take a *long hard look* at all this.

What we have here is:

<u>**In Step One**</u> - the combination together (by addition) of three numbers, the selection of which is based purely and simply on their status as the first three occurrences in **π** of the digit sequence <u>**17766771**</u> (a number which, in the form of a palindrome, symbolises, with awesome symmetry, in both the Biblical languages, the wonderful name of **JESUS** - see chapter 10); thus three numbers, each of which refers back specifically to the name "Jesus", are added together:

JESUS + JESUS + JESUS

<u>**In Step Two**</u> - a further combination (this time by multiplication with the last 8 digits of the first of those three occurrences) producing an even more specific and unmistakable identification of our calculation with that wonderful name:

(JESUS + JESUS + JESUS) x JESUS

<u>**In Step Three**</u> – the combination, by (subtraction / inversion), of the result of Step Two with **Key Point A** (which delimits the start of the **Encryption Zone**).

And finally[5] <u>**in Step Four**</u>, the simple doubling[6] of that result, to produce *both* the significant components of the "Superlative Palindrome" of chapter 10:

1776 **"JESUS, JESUS"** and

- 771 **"JESUS, JESUS"** [7] [8

Author's aside

What wonderful truths are now being revealed to us, if only our hearts, and minds, are willing to receive them!

CHAPTER 18

<u>Notes on chapter 18</u>:

(1) But actually (unknown to me when I originally wrote this) there are at least three different ways to generate <u>17766771</u> out of the Four Key Points, with pinpoint precision, all of which were only discovered some time after this chapter was written. Please refer to chapters 23 and 24.

(2) By "significant components", I mean the two digit-groups within 17766771 that make it so very special - 1776 and 771. As explained in chapter 10, "1776" symbolises the name "Jesus" because it is twice 888 ("Jesus" in Greek), and "771" also symbolises the name "Jesus" because it is as close to "772" (twice 386, "Jesus" in Hebrew) as the requirements of the palindromic form allow it to be. As the "6" between the two (1776 <u>6</u> 771), though certainly important, is arguably less important than the other digits in conveying the name Jesus to the reader, its absence from this particularly complex pattern can be readily understood. (For more on the palindrome, please turn to chapter 10, note 3). It should also be noted that as our result, 1776 2 771, is only 4,000 short of 1776 **<u>6</u>** 771, the difference between them (equivalent to one part in 4,442) is so miniscule as to leave no one (or at least no one of good sense and sound judgment) in any doubt as to the true intention and meaning of the pattern.

(3) This will be referred to as "Feature 16".

(4) This is the second of at least ten occasions where **Key Point B**, amazingly, provides a combination code which can be used as the key to unlock a deep pattern forming part of the Pi Encryption – similar to the "PIN" numbers and passwords with which we are all so familiar today. For more on this, please see chapter 21 ("The multi-purpose combination code").

(5) The probability of this result occurring randomly is calculated at 1 chance in 347,223, which is considerably less than one's chance of throwing 18 "heads" (or "tails") in 18 consecutive tosses of a coin, or of throwing 7 sixes in 7 consecutive throws of a dye. Yet, in order to avoid any suspicion of exaggeration, this very low probability has been dramatically increased, in the calculations contained in chapter 28, to 1 chance in 10, so as to skew the odds dramatically *against* the case for design which is at the heart of this book. For those who may like to know how the above probabilities were calculated (in (a) and (b), a binomial calculator was used):

(a) if selected randomly, the probability of 7 out of 8 digits matching their ordinal counterparts in a given 8 digit sequence (e.g. 1776<u>2</u>771 compared with 1776<u>6</u>771) is $7.2e^{-7}$, or 0.00000072, or one chance in 1,388,889;

(b) the chance of such a result occurring after 4 random attempts to achieve it (corresponding to the 4 "steps" described in this chapter) is 0.00000287999, or one chance in 347,223; and

(c) the chance of anyone throwing 18 "heads" (or 18 "tails") in 18 consecutive tosses of a coin is 0.5^{18}, or 0.00000381469, or one chance in 262,144; or of throwing 7 sixes in 7 consecutive throws of a dye is 0.166^{7}, or 0.0000035722, or one chance in 279,939.

(6) Doubling emphasises scale, majesty and truth, and 2 is one of the accepted step factors (see the Glossary).

(7) For an explanation of "771", please refer to chapter 10, note 3.

(8) This feature can be expressed by the following equation (where A, B, C and D represent the four Key Points). Note that, apart from 2 (which is an acceptable step factor – please refer to the Glossary), every single element in the calculation is one of the 4 Key Points:

$$2 \text{ x } (A - [(B + C + D) \text{ x } (\tfrac{B-A}{A})]) = \underline{\mathbf{1776}}_{2}\underline{\mathbf{771}}_{2.745}$$

(9) **Hallmarks of Design in chapter 18.**

Here we see **information and meaning** (**<u>1776</u>**(6)**<u>771</u>** = "Jesus", in the form of **Key Points B**, **C** and **D** - see chapter 10, note 9) being fed in at one end of a fearsome "mincing machine" of sums, with no logical reason to expect that it will come out, at the other end, as anything except a meaningless jumble of random digits. And yet, amazingly, that same and practically identical **information and meaning** (**<u>1776</u>**( )**<u>771</u>** = "Jesus") comes out, clear and undiluted, as the end-product of this incredible **systematic** process.

Not only that, but the metaphorical "mincing machine" itself is partly made up, as one if its main components, of the last 8 digits of **Key Point B**, as if to emphasise and highlight that very same significant **information and meaning**, so that no one (however reluctantly) can possibly fail to see it!

We also see, in Step 3, the essential involvement of **Key Point A**, without which (like all the other **Key Points**) this wonderful, elegant and sophisticated pattern simply would not exist.

But there is even more, and at a deeper level, for we see a profound **correspondence** at work between sections of Pi (in the digit-string **1776** (6) **771** at Step one) and their decimal place numbers in Pi (in **Key Points B**, **C** and **D**, also at Step one) from which the application of this **process** produces none other than - **1776**( )**771** in Step four! It is believed that this book is the first place where any such correspondences (for which no plausible explanation is possible, except deliberate design) have been reported. Further important examples are provided in chapter 20 and elsewhere.

CHAPTER 19

MIRROR IMAGE

How the name of **JESUS** is wonderfully reflected in **Key Point B**.

Introduction

We have seen in previous chapters how **Key Point B** (which, as you know, is at decimal place number 103,227186) is the very first occurrence in π of the digit-string 17766771, which itself (as we saw in chapter 10) palindromically represents 17766772 (twice **888_3386 – "Jesus, Jesus"**).

In this chapter, we shall be focusing on a most extraordinary characteristic of **Key Point B** – that it carries, embedded within itself, an exact "mirror image" of that very number from which its significance ultimately derives – 17766772!

First step

We simply take **Key Point B** (103227186) and remove its first two (1,0) and last two (8,6) digits, leaving:

32271

Second step

Next, we convert it into a palindrome, by reversing it (to make 17223) and putting the reversed digits immediately in front of it:

17223 32271

Third step

And to conclude, we invert it, to reveal our final result[1], thus:

$$\begin{array}{r} 1900000000 \\ -\ \ 1722332271 \\ \hline \mathbf{\underline{17766772}}_9 \end{array}$$

(twice $\mathbf{888_3386}$, "Jesus", "Jesus")

Note on chapter 19

(1) This will be referred to as "Feature 17".

CHAPTER 20

ECHOES

How the name of **JESUS** is miraculously "echoed" from one dimension of π to another, not just once, but twice, and how the two "echoes" *perfectly* complement each other.

1. Introduction

We are all familiar with *echoes*.

Imagine that you are standing at the top of an Alpine gorge, and that your mountain guide calls out a greeting, at the top of his voice, to a distant friend. A period elapses, perhaps a second or two, and suddenly you hear the guide's voice again, echoing off the mountainside opposite, almost as clearly as you heard it the first time.

Both sounds originated from your guide. In fact, they are both the same sound. The first was heard directly from him, the second indirectly, when it bounced back to your ears from the rock-face opposite.

Although the sound may not be quite as clear at the second hearing, *there is no doubt as to its origin.*

In this chapter, we shall be looking at two extraordinary "echoes" of the name of Jesus, each originating in the "**Digits of Pi**" (the mountain guide) and bounced back to us from the "**Digits between**" (the rock-face opposite).

2. The "Digits of Pi" and the "Digits between" – an explanation

There is a world of difference between these two.

They are both **dimensions** of π.

The "**Digits of Pi**" are the actual digits of **Pi** itself, starting at the beginning with 3.14159, and then going on forever, to infinity.

Each time the sequence **17766771** appears **in** Pi, it forms a tiny part **of** it. Its digits then are "Digits of Pi".

It occurs for the **first** time at decimal place numbers:

	103,227,186 which is a	**1**	
	103,227,187 which is a	**7**	
	103,227,188 which is a	**7**	
	103,227,189 which is a	**6**	the first **17766771** in π
	103,227,190 which is a	**6**	
	103,227,191 which is a	**7**	
	103,227,192 which is a	**7**	
and	103,227,193 which is a	**1**	

It occurs for the **second** time, with *exactly* 17,163,771 places between it and the first occurrence [(1)], at decimal place numbers:

	120,390,965 which is a	**1**	
	120,390,966 which is a	**7**	
	120,390,967 which is a	**7**	
	120,390,968 which is a	**6**	the second **17766771** in π
	120,390,969 which is a	**6**	
	120,390,970 which is a	**7**	
	120,390,971 which is a	**7**	
and	120,390,972 which is a	**1**	

and it occurs for the **third** time, with *precisely* 19,776,871 places between it and the first occurrence [(1)], at decimal place numbers:

	123,004,065 which is a	**1**	
	123,004,066 which is a	**7**	
	123,004,067 which is a	**7**	
	123,004,068 which is a	**6**	the third
	123,004,069 which is a	**6**	**<u>17766771</u>** in π
	123,004,070 which is a	**7**	
	123,004,071 which is a	**7**	
and	123,004,072 which is a	**1**	

These 3 separate occurrences of 17766771 are all parts of Pi itself, as they appear *within* it as *integral parts* of its decimal expansion - they are therefore "**Digits of Pi**".

However, the numbers we are calling "**Digits between**", are not parts of Pi, for, as the name suggests, they are arrived at by counting the number of decimal places of **Pi** which separate different occurrences of 17766771.

Thus, the **Digits between** the first and the second occurrences of 17766771 comprise decimal place numbers 103,227,194 to 120,390,964 inclusive, which, when counted, come to a total of *exactly* 17,163,771 digits.

And the **Digits between** the first and the third occurrences of 17766771 comprise decimal place numbers 103,227,194 to 123,004,064 inclusive, which, when counted, come to a total of *exactly* 19,776,871 digits.

It is these two "Digits between", 17,163,771 and 19,776,871, with which we have to deal when studying the wonderful "echoes" in Pi.

But before doing so, it is worth reminding ourselves that there is no *necessary*, or indeed *logical*, correlation or interplay between the **Digits of Pi** and the **Digits between**. They come from two completely separate and distinct enumerations, representing, as they do, entirely unrelated ideas. They are in fact entirely different *dimensions* of Pi. The one (**Digits of Pi**) is made up of small sections of π itself; whilst the other (**Digits between**) expresses the number of decimal places which separate two given **Digits of Pi**.

One should no more expect there to be any reciprocity, relationship, correspondence or interplay between them than between one's shoe size and the height of the Eiffel Tower!

And yet, as the following paragraphs demonstrate, there are clear and undeniable resonances - "echoes" - between the two: links so obvious and strong that only the *wilfully blind* could fail to acknowledge them.

3. Pinpoint accuracy

At this point, it is important to note how *exact* our calculations are.

There is no room for error, not even by a single digit.

The calculations are *precise,* so that the message may be *clear.*

There are *exactly* (not approximately) 17163771 decimal places between the first and the second occurrences in Pi of 17766771, and *exactly* (not approximately) 19776871 between the first and the third.

Only when it dawns on us how astronomically improbable such accuracy would be, in the absence of a Guiding Hand, can we begin to appreciate how truly remarkable the following patterns really are.

4. The first "echo" - 17766771 echoed by 19,776,871

The first of the wonderful "echoes" we have to consider is between 17766771 (the key to the **Pi Encryption**) and 19,776,871 (the **Digits between** the first and the third occurrences in **Pi** of the digit sequence 17766771).

We find it simply by writing the two sequences one above the other and comparing their corresponding digits, then seeing how many of them match, thus:

	1	7	**7**	6	**6**	7	**7**	**1**
	1	9	**7**	7	**6**	8	**7**	**1**
matches:	**1**	-	**7**	-	**6**	-	**7**	**1**

In this way, we see that no fewer than 5 out of the 8 corresponding pairs of digits are *matching pairs*!

To some, this may seem unremarkable. Yet, by the law of probability, the likelihood of this *echo pattern* occurring *randomly* (i.e. in the absence of deliberate design) can be accurately calculated (2) at no greater than **one chance in two thousand four hundred and forty-nine** (1:2,449).

In other words, the "echo" pattern we have before us(3) could only reasonably be expected to appear, on average, once in every 2,449 attempts to produce it, if all the attempts were haphazard, rather than by design.

5. The second "echo" - 17766771 echoed by 17163771

As you recall, 17766771 is the key to the **Pi Encryption** and 17,163,771 is the number of **Digits between** its first and second occurrences in **Pi**.

Following the same process we applied in section 4 produces an even more striking result:

	1	**7**	7	**6**	6	**7**	**7**	**1**
	1	**7**	1	**6**	3	**7**	**7**	**1**
matches:	**1**	**7**	-	**6**	-	**7**	**7**	**1**

No fewer than six - all but two - of the eight corresponding pairs of digits are *matching pairs*!

Here again, the chance of such an *echo pattern*[4] occurring *randomly*, by blind chance, can be accurately calculated[5], and it is no more than one chance in **forty-four thousand and ninety-two** (1:44,092).

And the likelihood of a "double echo" such as we have observed here (both echoes happening together in the same place and at the same time) can also be accurately calculated, simply by multiplying 2,449 (see section 4 above) by 44,092, a probability of only one chance in **one hundred and seven million, nine hundred and eighty-one thousand, three hundred and eight** (1:107,981,308).

So what this means, as a *scientific fact* (not merely a fanciful theory) is that the co-existence of these two interlocking and closely related echo patterns is well over 107 million times[6] *more* consistent with having been *deliberately designed,* than it is with having "just happened" by blind chance!

6. A synthesized echo - 17163771 and 19776871

Any investigating police detective will confirm that a single witness's statement is rarely a complete account of events. In order to build up a full picture of what happened, two or more witnesses may have to be interviewed. By collating, or synthesizing, their statements into one narrative, something approaching the full truth may be arrived at.

It is quite clear that neither of the "echoes" we are looking at - 17163771 and 19776871 - is by itself a *perfect* reproduction of the original "sound" - 17766771. But, by synthesizing the two of them together in a *systematic and orderly* way, can we reconstruct, perfectly and without flaw, the original "sound" of which they are both believed to be "echoes"?

If they were the product of *random* forces, one would surely not expect the answer to be "yes", as *system* and *order* are never to be found where *randomness* reigns!

But *are* they?

<u>First Synthesis</u>

Well, the only way to find out is to line them up and see[7]:

1 9 **7** 7 **6** 8 **7** 1 **First Echo**

1 **7** 1 **6** 3 **7** 7 **1** **Second Echo**

1 7 7 6 6 7 7 1 = **<u>"JESUS"</u>**

<u>Second Synthesis</u>

Or, in a different way[8]:

1 9 **7** 7 **6** 8 **7 1** **First Echo**

1 7 1 **6** 3 **7 7 1** **Second Echo**

1 7 7 6 6 7 7 1 = **<u>"JESUS"</u>**

We can clearly see, in both these cases, that by "synthesizing" the two "echoes", in a *systematic and orderly* way, then filtering out the discordant hum of background noise (the parts that are eliminated by the application of order), there is reconstructed before our very eyes a perfect "echo" of the original "sound" –

<u>17766771</u> -

NONE OTHER THAN THE WONDERFUL NAME OF JESUS!

Notes on chapter 20:

(1) As this is the number of digits *between* the two occurrences of 17766771, it includes no digit *forming part* of either of them. To illustrate this, although 10 minus 8 is 2, the number of digits *between* 8 and 10 is actually only one, namely 9.

(2) See Appendix 7. A chance of 1:2,449 is slightly less than one's chance of throwing 11 "heads" (or 11"tails") in 11 consecutive attempts – in other words, a very small chance indeed.

(3) This will be referred to as "Feature 18".

(4) This will be referred to as "Feature 19".

(5) See Appendix 8.

(6) Yet even this huge figure of over 107 million is not truly representative of the odds, as it takes no account of an important shared characteristic of both of the *echo patterns* with which we are dealing - that they are each based on 2 separate occurrences of 17766771. The true probability of such a double echo occurring *randomly*, taking **full** account of **all** the elements of the pattern, is actually only one chance in well over 10,000 trillion, trillion, trillion (see Appendix 9).

(7) By lining up the two "echoes" one above the other, and systematically selecting alternate digits from each of them in an orderly progression, we see, wonderfully reproduced before our very eyes, the original "sound" from which both the "echoes" originated – 17766771 ("Jesus" x 8 - see chapter 10, note 9). This will be referred to as "Feature 20".

(8) By lining up the two "echoes" one above the other, and systematically eliminating the digits in each line that do not correspond to their ordinal counterparts in 17766771 ("Jesus" x 8) we find, against extremely long odds, that each and every vertical column contains at least one (and in 3 cases two) corresponding digits. The probability of this happening, if all the digits are selected randomly, is $1:0.2^8$, or only one chance in 390,625 – substantially less than one's chance (which is one chance in 262,114) of tossing 18 heads (but no tails) or 18 tails (but no heads), in 18 consecutive tosses of a coin. This will be referred to as "Feature 21".

(9) **Hallmarks of Design in chapter 20**.

Perhaps the most striking hallmarks of design described in this chapter are the astonishing pinpoint **accuracy** noted in section 3 and the breathtaking **correspondence** between two logically unrelated dimensions (the **Digits of Pi** and the **Digits Between**) noted in sections 4-6. But we also see how the **significant grouping** of all 4 **Key Points** (with precise intervals between them) provides the basic data from which the echo patterns are formed, and the **orderly** way in which the two partly scrambled echoes in sections 4 and 5 can be refined and enhanced by the synthesizing processes described in section 6, so as to convey **information and meaning** in the end result, **17766771** ("Jesus, x 8" - see chapter 10, note 9). We also see how there is remarkable **consistency**, both between the data we start with in section 2 (**17766771** - "Jesus" x 8) and the two end results in section 6 (**17766771** - "Jesus" x 8) and also between the data presented in this chapter (**17766771** - "Jesus" x 8) and those presented throughout the remainder of this book (**17766771** - "Jesus" x 8). And, working deeply beneath the whole, at an unfathomable yet clearly perceptible level, we sense an all-pervading **purpose**, **system** and **process** at work to draw together, amalgamate and project all these wonderful phenomena to the glory of the **LORD GOD ALMIGHTY.**

CHAPTER 20

CHAPTER 21

THE MULTI-PURPOSE COMBINATION CODE

How Key Point B unlocks many doors that would otherwise remain forever shut.

It would be remiss of me not to shine a brief spotlight on one of the most interesting and, to me, convincing features of the Pi Encryption – one that defies any attempt to explain it away in naturalistic terms, and will persist undiminished, despite the most rigorous secular analysis, in its uncompromising proclamation of the Truth.

I wrote briefly before(1) about "*modus operandi*" – the specifically individual manner in which a creator, designer or artist of any kind characteristically goes about his work.

By identifying a specific "*modus operandi*" in a series of unattributed products (whether those products be works of art, consumer items, buildings or musical compositions), analysts can identify the artist, designer, builder or composer responsible for producing them, often with a high degree of accuracy.

One such "*modus operandi*" that is very evident in the Pi Encryption is the repeated use of Key Point B (or a section of it) as an essential link (whether by multiplication or division) to move from one stage of a calculation to the next.

We have already noted two such cases, in Features 9 ("the Golden Pathway" – chapter 11) and 16 ("Jesus, from Jesus, through Jesus" – chapter 18), and will see no fewer than eight more in chapter 22 – the second, fourth, fifth, sixth, eleventh, twelfth, thirteenth and fourteenth secret pathways.

The very existence of ten such uses is, in and of itself, a marvel beyond description, as it proves, (to everyone "with eyes to see") the existence of a common thread drawing all ten patterns (and, with them, all the other patterns with which they in turn are connected) into a single unified design – the brainchild of One who has power to place patterns in Pi!

Such elaborate patterns, as they are not alive, but exist only in the abstract world of mathematics, could not have "evolved" into existence by any natural process. If they exist at all (which is undeniable) they *must* have done so, complete and entire, from the very beginning of the universe.

In summary, the evidence shows that each of the following ten Features turns upon the use of Key Point B (or, in two cases, major sections of it), as an essential and precise element in its outworking(2):

(1) Feature 9 (chapter 11): 227186;

(2) Feature 16 (chapter 18): 03227186;

(3) Feature 23 (chapter 22): 103227186;

(4) Feature 25 (chapter 22): 103227186

(5) Feature 26 (chapter 22): 103227186;

(6) Feature 27 (chapter 22): 103227186;

(7) Feature 32 (chapter 22): 103227186;

(8) Feature 33 (chapter 22): 103227186;

(9) Feature 34 (chapter 22): 103227186; and

(10) Feature 35 (chapter 22): 103277186.

Key Point B is, in effect, a multi - purpose combination code, the existence of which defies any naturalistic explanation. It simply cannot have sprung up fortuitously, primed and ready for use, on so many occasions, out of a primeval state of chaos and disorder.

In light of all this, the conclusion may (indeed *must*) be drawn that the repeated use of Key Point B in this way amounts to compelling evidence that an individual *modus operandi* has been followed – in itself a hallmark of *intentional design* by one, supremely powerful, Intelligent Agent.

Should we not truly marvel, in amazement, that such an extraordinary phenomenon as this, which is absolutely impossible for secular minds to explain, should yet appear to us, in all its stark reality, as an *undeniable fact of nature*?

Notes on chapter 21

(1) See chapter 6, note 4. Three other *modi operandi* which appear to be very characteristic of the Designer of the Pi Encryption are : (a) the deduction of Key Point A (100,000,000) from all or some of the other Key Points, before using the remainders to form patterns (see, for instance, chapters 7, 11 and 14); (b) correspondences (see chapter 20, among others); and (c) the use of inversions.

(2) Just how remarkable this is may be judged by the fact that, *if selected at random*, the probability of any 9 digit sequence, such as 103227186, appearing anywhere at all, is at best only one chance in a billion. This is because there are exactly one billion different 9 digit sequences (from 000000000 to 999999999) to select from.

CHAPTER 21

CHAPTER 22

THE CROWNING GLORY
Part 1

Fourteen secret pathways - all leading to the Truth!

A. Introduction

I have placed this chapter (together with the following two, numbers 23 and 24) towards the end of the book, for two main reasons:

firstly, their contents would seem to be among the most important and wonderful of all; and

secondly, I only came across them late in the day, when all the other chapters had already been written!

The patterns described in these three extra chapters are so extraordinary as to justify a separate book of their own.

But as it would not be right for me to keep them from you now, I have tacked them on, near to the end of my previous work, by way of an addendum.

So please settle down to read about the "Crowning Glory" of everything found, so far, in the wonderful world of Pi!

B. A group apart, and three perfect reconciliations.

The "Crowning Glory" is made up of seventeen secret patterns, or pathways, of which: (1) the first 14, described in this chapter, though distinct from each other, form a natural group because (unlike the other patterns in the Pi Encryption), they are all based on **2614386**; (2) the fifteenth (described in chapter 23) provides a clear demonstration of the profound links between **386** ("Jesus"), the four Key Points, and **17766771**; and (3) the sixteenth and seventeenth (which are described in chapter 24) offer *both* a magnificent double reconciliation of **386**, **888**, **17766771**, and all four **Key Points**, *and* a fitting high point at which to conclude our exciting journey of exploration and discovery through the wonders of the Pi Encryption.

C. Why 2614386?

In a contest to find the best seven-digit combination of important messianic symbols, 2,614,386 would surely be a "hot favourite" to win!

In it, we see the harmonious amalgamation of five important numbers:

- **2,614,000** (an inversion of **386** and a well-spring of the Encryption – see the Preface);
- **614** (a shorter inversion of **386** commonly seen throughout this book);
- **386** ("Jesus" in Hebrew);
- **86** ("God" in Hebrew); and
- **614086** ("Jesus is God" – see chapter 9)

Anyone who acknowledges the reality of the **Pi Encryption** should not be surprised, therefore, to find that **2614386** is not only a sublime numerical expression of the name of Jesus, but is also the basis of fourteen extraordinary patterns, most of which are arguably just as impressive as any of the others described elsewhere in this book (except, possibly, for those in chapters 23 and 24).

D. A comparison

Have you ever looked inside a clock, or a watch?

Isn't it remarkable how the wheels, sprockets, levers, ratchets, gears and springs all work together in perfect unity, to produce a superbly accurate timepiece?

Each of the many parts has been meticulously crafted to complement the others, so as to harness motive power and convert it efficiently into readable information.

The precise weight, shape and size of each of them, as well as its exact position with regard to the others, are all crucial to the operation of the mechanism.

Separately, they are no more than a jumble of parts, incapable of achieving any useful purpose.

Assembled, their finely tuned collaboration is not only a wonder to behold, but also of great benefit and utility to mankind.

But if the least of them is removed, damaged or displaced, even by a tiny fraction, the clock will lose or gain time, or even stop completely.

It is this image of **superb harmony** and **rigorously efficient design** that I would ask you to keep constantly in mind, as we explore the following sections of this chapter.

E. An impossible task, and ten essential components

At the heart of this chapter is a seemingly impossible task – to discover how ten very different, and apparently ill-matched, numerical **components** have been engineered together into not one, two, or even three, but fourteen, distinct, precision tooled, efficiently functioning and perfectly integrated systems, each of them just like the timepiece we considered in section D.

Fourteen interlocking, but independent, mathematical processes that are robust and repeatable, reversible and reconcilable, revealing, relevant and irrefutable.

And our aim is, by seeking out and finding these *literally* impossible (and therefore, of necessity, *supernatural*) manifestations of God's power, to catch in them just a hint, however fleeting, of that **Crowning Glory**, the full and eternal enjoyment of which is promised to all true Gospel believers.

These ten **essential components** are, as might be expected, those important elements of the Pi Encryption which we have already discussed, (in most cases, many times) earlier in this book:

- **386** - "Jesus" in Hebrew;
- **2,614,386** - see section C above;
- **17766771** the key to the Pi Encryption;
- **17766772** the original length of the First Section (see the Preface);
- **17766888** a combination of 1776 (twice 888 - "Jesus", "Jesus") and 888 ("Jesus") – see chapter 17:
- **17,777,865** - the adjusted length of the First Section (see the Preface);
- **100,000,000** - Key Point A;
- **103,227,186** - Key Point B;
- **120,390,965** - Key Point C; and
- **123,004,065** - Key Point D.

No matter how hard you may try, I do not think you will ever be able to assemble all of these ten **essential components** into fourteen fully integrated and mutually complementary working systems, comparable to the clock mechanism we considered in section D –

Unless that is, you follow the **fourteen secret pathways** that we are about to explore.

F. The Fourteen Pathways

So numerous are the Pathways to be described in this chapter, that the task of presenting them to you in a reasonably digestible form, and without unduly testing your patience, has given me considerable pause for thought.

The course I have decided on is to rely mainly on diagrams, rather than verbal descriptions. I hope this will enable you to see the patterns clearly, without being distracted by too many words.

In the following pages, these symbols have been used:

"A"	(key point A)	=	100,000,000
"B"	(key point B)	=	103,227,186
"C"	(key point C)	=	120,390,965
"D"	(key point D)	=	123,004,065
"F"	(the length of the **F**irst Section)	=	17,777,865
"Y"	the result of the last preceding calculation.		

G. The First Secret Pathway

2614386
"JESUS"

	1	2
	$\frac{Y}{50}$	F - Y
	3	4
	$\frac{Y}{400}$	D – (C+Y)
	5	6
	$Y \div \left(\frac{D-A}{A}\right)$	A – Y
	7	
	Y x 20	

= **1776**$_{66}$**6771**.$_{12936}$
"JESUS"

Comments:

(1) Apart from the three step factors 20, 50 and 400, *all* the numbers included in this First Pathway are among the ten **essential components** listed in section E.

(2) The extra two sixes in the result (1776<u>66</u>6771) are not a weakness, but a strength, of this pattern, as they correspond exactly to those on either side of them, and thereby complement and confirm, rather them detracting from, its essential integrity. They could so easily have been two quite different digits, each as a 0 and an 8, or a 2 and a 5, which would have borne no continuity or affinity with their neighbours on either side, and would therefore have destroyed the flawless symmetry of the pattern. 1776<u>66</u>6771 is still a perfect palindrome, just like 17766771, which it clearly represents in this Pathway.

(3) This Pathway is strikingly analogous to the Tenth Pathway (see comment 2 in Section P).

(4) This First Secret Pathway will be referred to as "Feature 22".

H. The Second Secret Pathway

<u>**2614386**</u>
"<u>**JESUS**</u>"

1	2
$\frac{Y}{50}$	F - Y
3	4
$\frac{Y}{400}$	$Y + \left(\frac{D-A}{5{,}000}\right)$
5	6
Y + (D-A)	$\frac{Y}{B}$
7	8
$Y \times \left(\frac{A}{10}\right)$	$\left(\frac{A}{5}\right) - Y$

= <u>**17766772**</u>.4318
"<u>**JESUS**</u>"

Comments:

(1) Apart from the five step factors 5, 10, 50, 400 and 5,000, *all* the numbers included in this Pathway are among the ten **essential components** listed in section E.

(2) The result (17766772) is, of course, twice **8883386**, and, as such, one of the basic foundations of the Pi Encryption, the key to which (17766771) is its near neighbour and palindromic alter ego (please see the Preface and chapter 10, note 3, for more on this).

(3) This (along with the fourth, fifth, sixth, eleventh, twelfth, thirteenth and fourteenth secret pathways) is one of the many places in the Pi Encryption where the digits of Key Point B (103227186) are used as a precise combination code (see chapter 21).

(4) This Second Secret Pathway will be referred to as "Feature 23".

I. The Third Secret Pathway

2614386
"JESUS"

1: $\frac{Y}{50}$	2: Y x 10
3: Y - $\left(\frac{386}{10}\right)$	4: Y + F
5: Y - $\left(\frac{386}{10}\right)$	6: Y - 17766888
7: $\left(\frac{A}{20}\right)$ - Y	8: $\frac{Y}{2}$
9: $\left(\frac{A}{5}\right)$-Y	

= $1776_{6}888._{50}$
"JESUS"

Comments:

(1) Apart from the five step factors 2, 5, 10, 20 and 50, *all* the numbers included in this Pathway are to be found among the ten **essential components** listed in section E.

(2) The four appearances of **386** ("Jesus" in Hebrew-three times as itself, and a fourth time - in its inverted form of 614 - in 2**614**386), as well as of the very result (**1776**6**888**) ("Jesus, Jesus, Jesus") as an essential element in its own calculation, are all of very great interest, and surely cannot be shrugged off as mere coincidences.

(3) Just as **386** and **1776**6**888** are both essential elements, in this Pathway, in the formation of **1776**6**888**, so **386** and **17766772** are both essential elements, in the Seventh Pathway, in the formation of **17766772**.

(4) In this, as in the first, second, seventh, tenth, eleventh, twelfth, thirteenth and fourteenth Pathways, "F" (the length of the First Section, 17777865) plays a vital role – no fewer than 11 appearances in all (including 2 each in the tenth and eleventh Pathways alone).

(5) This Third Secret Pathway will be referred to as "Feature 24".

J. The Fourth Secret Pathway

2614386
"**JESUS**"

1	2
$\frac{Y}{50}$	$Y - \left(\frac{C}{100{,}000}\right)$
3	**4**
$\left(\frac{A}{1{,}000}\right) - Y$	$Y + (D\text{-}A)$
5	**6**
$\frac{Y}{B}$	$Y \times \left(\frac{A}{10}\right)$
7	**8**
$\left(\frac{A}{5}\right) - Y$	

= **17766772**.2929
"**JESUS**"

Comments:

(1) Apart from the five step factors 5, 10, 50, 1,000 and 100,000, *all* the numbers included in this Pathway are to be found among the **essential components** listed in section E.

(2) In this, and Pathways six, thirteen and fourteen, all four Key Points (A,B,C and D) feature together.

(3) This (along with the second, fifth, sixth, eleventh, twelfth, thirteenth and fourteenth secret pathways) is one of the many places in the Pi Encryption where the digits of Key Point B (103227186) are used as a precise combination code (see chapter 21).

(4) The tiny remainder of 0.2929 means that this calculation is accurate to one part in over sixty million.

(5) This Fourth Secret Pathway will be referred to as "Feature 25"

K. The Fifth Secret Pathway

2614386
"JESUS"

1	2
$\frac{Y}{50}$	$\left(\frac{A}{1{,}000}\right) - Y$
3	**4**
$Y + (D-A)$	$\frac{Y}{B}$
5	**6**
$Y \times \left(\frac{A}{10}\right)$	$\left(\frac{A}{5}\right) - Y$

= **1776**$_{6}$**888**.$_{9201}$
"JESUS"

Comments:

(1) Apart from the four step factors 5, 10, 50 and 1,000, *all* the numbers included in this Pathway are to be found among the ten **essential components** listed in section E.

(2) As in Pathways two, four, six, eleven, twelve, thirteen and fourteen, Key Point A appears no fewer than 4 times in this Pathway.

(3) This (along with the second, fourth, sixth, eleventh, twelfth, thirteenth and fourteenth secret pathways) is one of the many places in the Pi Encryption where the digits of Key Point B (103227186) are used as a precise combination code (see chapter 21).

(4) The tiny remainder of 0.9201 means that this calculation is accurate to one part in over nineteen million.

(5) The Fifth Secret Pathway will be referred to as "Feature 26".

L. The Sixth Secret Pathway

2614386
"JESUS"

Step	Operation	Step	Operation
1	$\frac{Y}{50}$	2	$\left(\frac{A}{1{,}000}\right) - Y$
3	Y + (D-A)	4	$\frac{Y}{B}$
5	A x Y	6	Y x 20

= **446622216**
(or A + B + C + D)
"JESUS"

Comments:

(1) Apart from the three step factors 20, 50 and 1,000, *all* the numbers included in this Pathway are among the ten essential **components** listed in section E.

(2) Despite sharing its first four steps with the fifth pathway, a dramatically different result is obtained.

(3) This (along with the second, fourth, fifth, eleventh, twelfth, thirteenth and fourteenth secret pathways) is one of the many places in the Pi Encryption where the digits of Key Point B (103227186) are used as a precise combination code (see chapter 21).

(4) The exact result is 446,622,215.973222, which falls short of 446,622,216 by only 0.02677, and means that the calculation is accurate to one part in over sixteen billion.

(5) This Sixth Secret Pathway will be referred to as "Feature 27".

M. The Seventh Secret Pathway

<u>2614386</u>
"<u>JESUS</u>"

Step	Operation	Step	Operation
1	$\frac{Y}{50}$	2	Y x 10
3	Y + F	4	$Y - \left(\frac{386}{10}\right)$
5	Y - 386	6	Y - 17766772
7	$\left(\frac{A}{20}\right) - Y$	8	$\frac{Y}{2}$
9	$\left(\frac{A}{5}\right) - Y$		

= <u>17766772</u>.8
"<u>JESUS</u>"

Comments:

(1) Apart from the five step factors 2, 5, 10, 20 and 50, *all* the numbers included in this Pathway are among the ten **essential components** listed in section E.

(2) This calculation has the amazing characteristic of having, as one of its **essential components**, the very number

(17766772) which is its end result – as well as 386 (four times – thrice as itself and once in its inverted form of 614), the length of the First Section (17777865) and Key Point A (twice). See comment 3 in Section N below.

(3) The tiny remainder of 0.8 means that this calculation is accurate to one part in over twenty-two million.

(4) This Seventh Secret Pathway will be referred to as "Feature 28".

N. The Eighth Secret Pathway

2614386
"JESUS"

1	2
Y x 7	Y - 386
3	**4**
Y - 17766772	$\left(\frac{A}{20}\right) - Y$
5	**6**
$\frac{Y}{2}$	$\left(\frac{A}{5}\right) - Y$

= 17766772
"JESUS"

Comments:

(1) This is the first of the seven Pathways – one half of them – that commence not with (2614386 ÷ 50), as in the first seven, but with (2614386 x 7).

(2) Apart from the 4 step factors 2, 5, 7 and 20, *all* the numbers included in this Pathway are to be found amongst the ten **essential components** listed in section E.

(3) A remarkable feature here, as in the Seventh Pathway, is that both **386** ("Jesus" in Hebrew) and **17766772** (twice **8883386**, "Jesus" in both Greek and Hebrew) are essential elements in this calculation, the result of which incredibly is

none other than **17766772** itself – to say nothing of the triple appearance of **386** (twice as itself and once again in its inverted form 614 in 2**614**386). Compare this with the Third and Ninth Pathways (in Sections I and O), where similar marvels are to be found, but this time involving **386** and **1776**6**888**. Can such a long string of uncanny coincidences really have arisen purely by chance? Wouldn't to suggest such a thing be verging on the absurd?

(4) As this result (17766772) is absolutely exact, having no remainder or shortfall whatsoever, it has an accuracy of 100%.

(5) This Eighth Secret Pathway will be referred to as "Feature 29".

O. The Ninth Secret Pathway

2614386
"JESUS"

1	2
Y x 7	$Y - \left(\frac{386}{10}\right)$
3	**4**
Y - 17766888	$\left(\frac{A}{20}\right) - Y$
5	**6**
$\frac{Y}{2}$	$\left(\frac{A}{5}\right) - Y$

= **17766888**
"JESUS"

Comments:

(1) Apart from the five step factors 2, 5, 7, 10 and 20, *all* the numbers included in this calculation are to be found amongst the ten **essential components** listed in section E.

(2) Once again (as in the Third Pathway) **1776**6**888** ("Jesus, Jesus, Jesus") appears not only as the *result* of this

calculation, but also, along with **386** ("Jesus" in Hebrew, appearing three times, twice as itself, and once in its inverted form 614) as *an* ***essential component*** *in its own calculation.* Please see comment 3 in Section N above for more examples of this extraordinary phenomenon.

(3) The exact result is 17766887.70, which falls short of 17766888 by 0.30, and means that the calculation is accurate to one part in over fifty-nine million.

(4) This Ninth Secret Pathway will be referred to as "Feature 30".

P. The Tenth Secret Pathway

2614386
“**JESUS**”

Step	Operation	Step	Operation
1	Y x 7	2	Y - F
3	$\frac{Y}{10}$	4	F - Y
5	$\frac{Y}{400}$	6	D – (C + Y)
7	$Y \div \left(\frac{D-A}{A}\right)$	8	A - Y
9	Y x 20		

= **1776**66**6772**.003124
"**JESUS**"

Comments:

(1) Apart from the four step factors 7, 10, 20 and 400, *all* the numbers included in this Pathway are among the ten **essential components** listed in section E.

(2) This calculation is strikingly analogous to the First Pathway, although it starts with (2614386 x 7) instead of (2614386 ÷ 50), and ends with $1776_{66}6772$ instead of $1776_{66}6771$.

(3) The double appearance of "F" (17777865) is a striking feature of this secret pathway, as it is in the Eleventh Pathway, and (along with the several other appearances of "F" in the other Pathways) conclusively proves the significance of the First Section as one of the principal structural divisions of the Encryption Zone (as explained in the Preface).

(4) This Tenth Secret Pathway will be referred to as "Feature 31".

Q. The Eleventh Secret Pathway

2614386
"JESUS"

Step		Step	
1	Y x 7	2	Y - F
3	$\frac{Y}{10}$	4	F - Y
5	$\frac{Y}{400}$	6	$Y + \left(\frac{D-A}{5{,}000}\right)$
7	Y + (D - A)	8	$\frac{Y}{B}$
9	$Y \times \left(\frac{A}{10}\right)$	10	$\left(\frac{A}{5}\right) - Y$

= **17766772.**4308
"JESUS"

Comments:

(1) Apart from the five step factors 5, 7, 10, 400 and 5,000 *all* the numbers included in this Pathway are among the ten **essential components** listed in section E.

(2) This (along with the second, fourth, fifth, sixth, twelfth, thirteenth and fourteenth secret pathways) is one of the many places in the Pi Encryption where the digits of Key Point B (103227186) are used as a precise combination code (see chapter 21).

(3) The double appearance of "F" (17777865) is a striking feature of this secret pathway, as it is in the Tenth Pathway.

(4) This Eleventh Secret Pathway will be referred to as "Feature 32".

R. The Twelfth Secret Pathway

2614386
"**JESUS**"

1	2
Y x 7	Y - F
3	4
$\frac{Y}{10}$	$\left(\frac{A}{1000}\right)$ - Y
5	6
Y + (D - A)	$\frac{Y}{B}$
7	8
Y x $\left(\frac{A}{10}\right)$	$\left(\frac{A}{5}\right)$ - Y

= $\underline{1776}_{6}\underline{888}.5307$
"**JESUS**"

Comments:

(1) Apart from the four step factors 5, 7, 10 and 1000, *all* the numbers included in this Pathway are among the ten **essential components** listed in section E.

(2) This (along with the second, fourth, fifth, sixth, eleventh, thirteenth and fourteenth secret pathways), is one of the many places in the Pi Encryption where the digits of Key Point B (103227186) are used as a precise combination code (see chapter 21).

(3) In this Pathway, the double appearance within 2,614,386, of **<u>386</u>** ("Jesus") – firstly in its inverted form 614 and then as itself, *<u>in Hebrew</u>* – is instrumental, via combinations with the length of the First Section and Key Points A, B and D, in producing both **<u>1776</u>** ("Jesus, Jesus") and **<u>888</u>** ("Jesus"), *<u>in Greek</u>*.

(4) This Twelfth Secret Pathway will be referred to as "Feature 33".

<u>S. The Thirteenth Secret Pathway</u>

<u>2614386</u>
"<u>JESUS</u>"

	1	2
	$Y \times 7$	$Y - F$
	3	4
	$\frac{Y}{10}$	$Y - \left(\frac{C}{100{,}000}\right)$
	5	6
	$\left(\frac{A}{1{,}000}\right) - Y$	$Y + (D - A)$
	7	8
	$\frac{Y}{B}$	$Y \times \left(\frac{A}{10}\right)$
	9	
	$\left(\frac{A}{5}\right) - Y$	

= <u>17766772</u>
"<u>JESUS</u>"

Comments:

(1) Apart from the five step factors 5, 7, 10, 1,000 and 100,000, *all* the numbers included in this Pathway are among the ten **essential components** listed in section E.

(2) This (along with the second, fourth, fifth, sixth, eleventh, twelfth and fourteenth secret pathways), is one of the many places in the Pi Encryption where the digits of Key Point B (103227186) are used as a precise combination access code (see chapter 21).

(3) The exact result of this calculation is 17766771.9035, which falls short of 17766772 by 0.09649, and is accurate therefore to one part in over 184 million.

(4) This Thirteenth Secret Pathway will be referred to as "feature 34".

T. The Fourteenth Secret Pathway

2614386
"JESUS"

Step	Operation	Step	Operation
1	$Y \times 7$	2	$Y - F$
3	$\frac{Y}{10}$	4	$Y + 4$
5	$\left(\frac{A}{1{,}000}\right) - Y$	6	$Y + (D - A)$
7	$\frac{Y}{B}$	8	$A \times Y$
9	$Y \times 20$		

= **446,622,216**.360716
(A + B + C + D)
"JESUS"

Comments:

(1) Apart from the five step factors 4,7,10,20 and 1,000 *all* the numbers included in this Pathway are among the ten ***essential components*** listed in section E.

(2) This (along with the second, fourth, fifth, sixth, eleventh, twelfth and thirteenth secret pathways) is one of the many places in the Pi Encryption where the digits of Key Point B (103227186) are used as a precise combination code (see chapter 21).

(3) This Fourteenth Secret Pathway will be referred to as "feature 35".

U. The Fourteen Secret Pathways

As it may not be immediately apparent to everyone, from the diagrams and comments contained in the last few pages, just how extremely *interconnected* the Fourteen Secret Pathways are, and how they all form different, yet mutually *corresponding*, motifs in a single grand design (just like the clock parts mentioned in section D), please refer to the colour-coded diagram on the next page, which should be of some assistance to you in gauging just how heavily imprinted these patterns are with all the most striking and indisputable **hallmarks of design**.

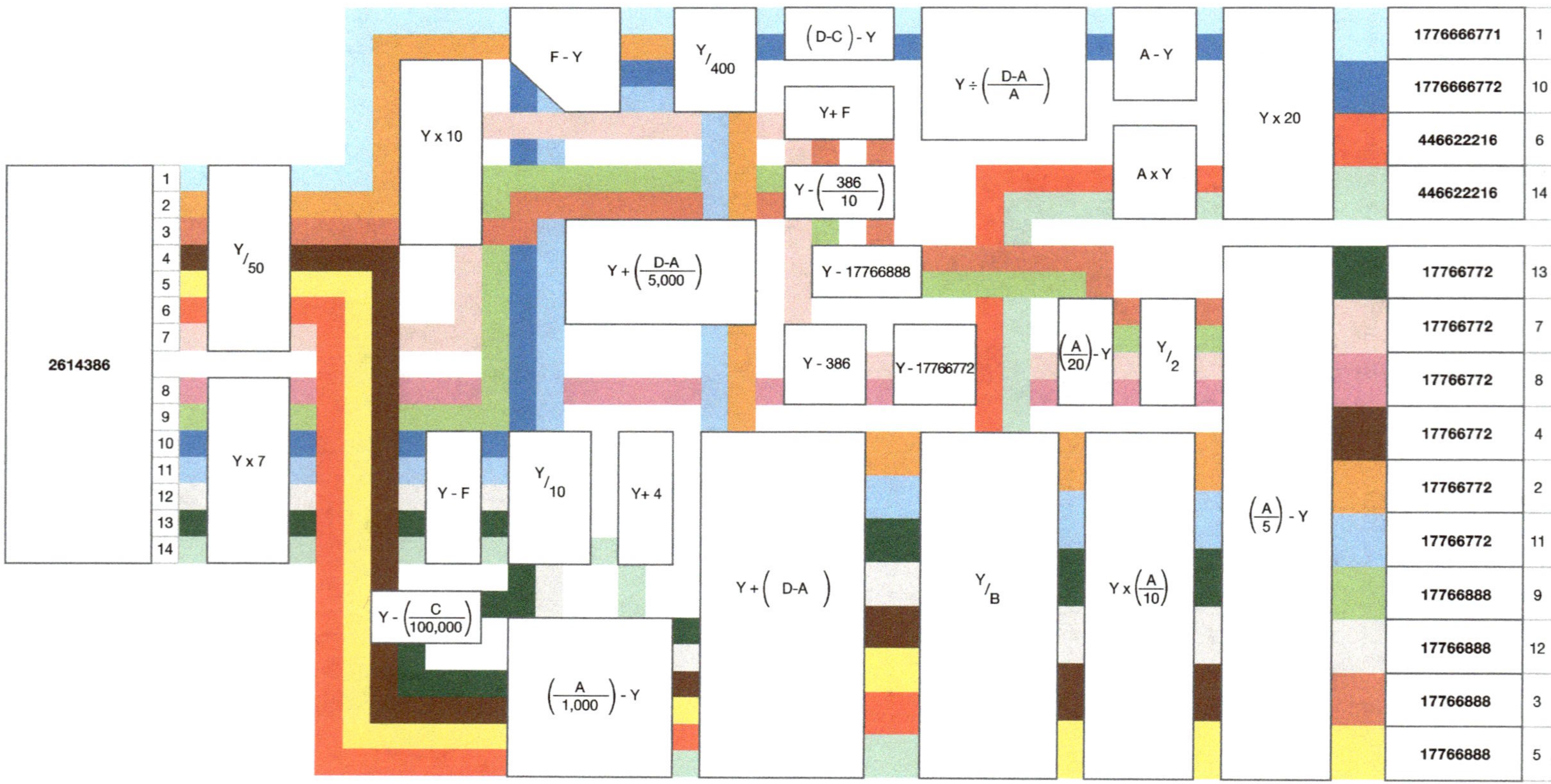

2614386
1
2
3
4
5
6
7
8
9
10
11
12
13
14
Y/50
Y x 7
Y x 10
F - Y
Y - F
Y/10
Y+ 4
Y - (C/100,000)
(A/1,000) - Y
Y/400
Y + ((D-A)/5,000)
(D-C) - Y
Y+ F
Y - (386/10)
Y - 17766888
Y - 386
Y - 17766772
Y + (D-A)
Y ÷ ((D-A)/A)
A - Y
A x Y
(A/20) - Y
Y/2
Y/B
Y x (A/10)
Y x 20
(A/5) - Y
1776666771 1
1776666772 10
446622216 6
446622216 14
17766772 13
17766772 7
17766772 8
17766772 4
17766772 2
17766772 11
17766888 9
17766888 12
17766888 3
17766888 5

Notes on the diagram opposite:

(1) Each of the Fourteen Secret Pathways is shown in a different distinctive colour.

(2) Starting on the left with **2614386**, follow each pathway (by its distinctive colour) from box to box, finishing on the right hand side of the diagram.

(3) In each case where it occurs, "y" stands for the result of the calculation in the box immediately before it.

(4)

A	=	Key Point A	(100,000,000)
B	=	Key Point B	(103,227,186)
C	=	Key Point C	(120,390,965)
D	=	Key Point D	(123,004,065)
F	=	First Section	(17,777,865)

(5) You will see that each pathway ends in a result which is deeply symbolic of the name "Jesus", as it is one or more of the following:

(1) 17766771 the key to the Pi Encryption (see chapter 10);

(2) 17766772 twice **8888386** (see the Preface, chapter 10 and chapter 19);

(3) 446622216 the sum of all four Key Point (see chapter 17); and

(4) 17766888 "Jesus, Jesus, Jesus" (see chapter 17).

Hallmarks of Design in the Fourteen Secret Pathways

(1) **Symmetry**. There are fourteen pathways, of which exactly one half start with (2,614,386 ÷ 50) and the other half with (2,614,386 x 7).

(2) **Convergences**. There are 27 calculation boxes, of which all but one are visited more than once, showing a remarkable degree of *convergence*. One of them is visited 10 times, two of them 8 times, two of them 7 times, one of them 6 times, three of them 5 times, and five of them 4 times.

(3) **Mutual Reciprocity**. In pathway three, the result (17766888) is arrived at by a combination of 386, Key Point A and 17766888 itself, whilst in Pathway 7, the result (17766772) is arrived at by a combination of 386, Key Point A and 17766772 itself – a remarkable degree of *mutual reciprocity* between the 2 Pathways.

(4) **Corresponding Process**. No fewer than 10 out of the 14 Pathways end in the same box, ($\left(\frac{A}{5}\right)$ – y) and the other four all end in box (y x 20).

(5) **Computational Efficiency**. The Pathways are all completed after visiting 6 – 10 calculation boxes each, with an average of only 7.79. The likelihood that 14 exact and mutually congruent results of the kind found here could be arrived at, with such *computational efficiency*, using 10 numerical components which had been *selected at random* (rather than the ten **essential components** listed in section E), is vanishingly small.

(6) **Complex Combination Coding**. In no fewer than eight out of the fourteen pathways (numbers 2, 4, 5, 6, 11, 12, 13 and 14), all eight digits of Key Point A (103227186) are used

as a precise and *complex combination code*. Compare this to your bank "PIN" code, which, although it is characteristically only 4 digits long, is considered a strong enough encryption to guard your account against unauthorised access.

(7) **Thematic Consistency**. All 14 results, as well as the number with which all the pathways begin (2 **614** **386**) are entirely *consistent with*, and *supportive of* the overall *theme* of the Encryption – to honour and exalt the name of **JESUS**.

(8) **Pinpoint Precision**. Although all the results of the secret pathways (with the exception of number 8) have slight remainders or shortfalls, as these are all less than one, the expression "*pinpoint precision*" (as defined in the Glossary) can fairly be applied to them. As the Eighth Secret Pathway has no remainder or shortfall at all, (as well as being among the most direct, visiting only 6 calculation boxes along its entire length), it may justly be regarded as the purest, most perfect, and therefore most significant, of them all.

(9) **Information and Meaning**. As both the number 2 **614** **386** with which all the pathways start, and each and every result to which the pathways lead, (as well of course as the majority of the elements of which the calculations themselves are composed) are all easily capable, without any overuse of one's imaginative faculties, of symbolically representing the name "Jesus", it would be nothing short of perverse to deny the *information and meaning* that the pathways are clearly intended to convey.

(10) **Order (prismatic refraction)**.
Just as a prism refracts sunlight into the seven colours of the rainbow, so each of the first two calculation boxes (via the complex combinations of the pathways which stem from it) filters 2**614** **386**, (an unmistakable symbol of **Jesus**),

into seven more unmistakable numerical symbols of that same great name. Each of these symbols is perfectly matched by a corresponding image from the other prism, as in both groups there are four representations of 17766771(2), two of 17766888 and one of 446622216. How can one possibly explain the existence of such exquisite *order*, except as a clear and obvious *hallmark of design*?

CHAPTER 23

THE CROWNING GLORY - Part II

"A HEAVENLY PATHWAY"

How **386** can be combined with the Four Key Points to produce, in nine easy steps, the *exact* key to the Pi Encryption.

In this chapter, we shall be considering whether it is possible, in just a few easy steps, to chart a precise mathematical course between **386** ("Jesus" in Hebrew) and **17766771** (the key to the Pi Encryption), using only **386** ("Jesus" in Hebrew), the four key points, and a few basic step factors, such as 5, 10 and 100.

Our purpose in doing this is to prove, once again, that there exists a strong and undeniable affinity between these six numbers, which can only be explained by the presence of a deep underlying plan.

Like both of the similar patterns in the next chapter, this one[(1)] has 9 separate stages, or steps, each of which is as simple and straightforward as it is possible to imagine:

The first step

is to multiply Key Point A by 10:
100,000,000 x 10 = 1,000,000,000

The second step

is to divide Key Point A by 5:
100,000,000 ÷ 5 = 20,000,000

The third step

is to divide Key Point A by 100:
100,000,000 ÷ 100 = 1,000,000

The fourth step

is to add all four Key Points together:

A	100,000,000
B	103,227,186
C	120,390,965
D	123,004,065
	446,622,216

The fifth step

is to divide the result of the first step by **386** ("Jesus" in Hebrew):

$$\frac{1,000,000,000}{386} = 2,590,673.57513$$

The sixth step

is to subtract the result of the fifth step from the result of the first step:

1,000,000,000 – 2,590,673.57513 = 997,409,326.42487

The seventh step

is to divide the result of the sixth step by the result of the fourth step:

$$\frac{997{,}409{,}326.42487}{446{,}622{,}216} = 2.233228197553$$

The eighth step

is to multiply the result of the seventh step by the result of the third step:

2.233228197553 x 1,000,000 = 2,233,228.197553

and

The ninth step

is to subtract the result of the eighth step from the result of the second step:

20,000,000 – 2,233,228.197553 = **17766771**.802
(see note 2)

How truly remarkable it is that all these numbers (the significance of three of which, Key Points B, C and D, derives solely from their status as the first three iterations of 17766771 in Pi) should fit together so easily and well, together with 386 ("Jesus" in Hebrew), to produce, with *pinpoint precision*, the same great number – 17766771 – from which that significance is derived!

Just how exquisitely precise this all is may be judged by the fact that only by the use of 386, at the fifth step, can a meaningful result be achieved at all. Substitute 385 or 387 for it, and the end result will be more than 14 over, or under, our otherwise unachievable goal of *exactly* 17766771.

Could *anyone* produce, *by merely random selection*, another set of six numbers capable of generating such a perfect, precise and unimpeachable *pattern*?

Found, as it is, in such a place as Pi, and even without regard to all the other wonders described in this book, this "Heavenly Pathway" is, in this author's humble opinion, fully worthy to be described as "a miracle".

It is shown, in the form of an equation, in the diagram on the next page(3).

"A HEAVENLY PATHWAY"

from **386** ("Jesus" in Hebrew) to **17766771**
using only 386 itself, the four Key Points, 5, 10 and 100

$$\left(\frac{A}{5}\right) - \left[\left(\frac{10A - \left(\frac{A \times 10}{386}\right)}{A + B + C + D}\right) \times \left(\frac{A}{100}\right)\right] = \mathbf{17766771}_{.802}$$

A	=	100,000,000	the 4 Key Points
B	=	103,227,186	
C	=	120,390,965	
D	=	123,004,065	

Notes on chapter 23

(1) It will be referred to as "feature 36"

(2) The tiny remainder of 0.802 means that this calculation is accurate to one part in well over 22,000,000.

(3) Using the known mathematical relationship between 23004065 (the length of the Encryption Zone) 386 ("Jesus" in Hebrew) and 888 ("Jesus" in Greek) – see chapter 14 – it is possible to adapt feature 36 to show an almost identical pathway from 888 to 17766771, as follows:

$$\left(\frac{A}{5}\right) - \left(\frac{10A - \left(\frac{D - A}{888} \times 100\right)}{A + B + C + D} \times \frac{A}{100}\right) = \underline{\mathbf{17766771}}.52096$$

However, as this may be said to be merely a fusion of part of feature 2 with feature 36, and in the interests of maintaining this book's core policy of always *understating* the case for the Pi Encryption, it will not be given its own independent feature number here.

It is, nonetheless, a most interesting and elegant equation, the likes of which simply could not have arisen, unplanned, out of randomness, disorder and confusion.

(4) **Hallmarks of Design in chapter 23**

In feature 36 we see at work, once again, that extraordinary **correspondence**, unique to the Pi Encryption, between precise decimal place numbers in Pi (represented by Key Points B, C and D) on the one hand, and, on the other, the exact corresponding digits of Pi (17766771) by which they are identified.

We also see, once again, how the strong **affinity** between 386 ("Jesus" in Hebrew) and 17766771 works, in conjunction with the four Key Points, to form a **perfectly balanced** and **orderly reconciliation**, which is completely **consistent** with, and therefore **corroborative** of, the other proofs presented in this book.

CHAPTER 24

THE CROWNING GLORY - Part III

A chapter to convince even the most sceptical readers.

1. Introduction

This chapter is addressed primarily to the most sceptical readers - those who, even at this late stage in the book, remain unconvinced that the Pi Encryption really exists.

What evidence must this chapter contain to finally convince you of its reality?

Wouldn't you have to see a set of patterns containing such a long and orderly string of "coincidences" as to eliminate any thought, even in *your* sceptical mind, that they might have arisen by chance?

In this chapter we shall discuss what I personally consider to be the most convincing pattern (or rather pair of patterns) of all – one that arguably amounts to a stand-alone proof, "beyond reasonable doubt", of the Pi Encryption's truth and reality.

2. The task we are setting ourselves: to plot two independent courses to 17766771

As we all know by now, the three most important numbers underpinning the Pi Encryption are 386 ("Jesus" in Hebrew), 888 ("Jesus" in Greek) and 17766771 (the key to the Pi Encryption).

Next in importance are the four Key Points, 100,000,000, 103,227,186, 120,390,965 and 123,004,065, about which we have already heard so much in the preceding chapters.

Now, imagine that you are asked to plot a mathematical course from 386 to 17766771, using only 386 itself, the 4 Key Points, 10 and 1,000.

And that you are also asked to plot another similar mathematical course, this time from 888 to 17766771, using only 888 itself, the 4 Key Points, 10 and 1,000.

Both courses must have exactly the same number of steps, each of which must mirror exactly, or be very similar to, the corresponding step in the other course.

You can only use the simplest mathematical "tools" that exist – addition, subtraction, multiplication and division. Nothing more sophisticated or technical is permitted.

But, in each case, the course must be plotted with *absolute* accuracy and *pinpoint* precision, as no approximations whatsoever will be allowed, even to make a fair allowance for the simplicity and lack of sophistication of the "tools" you are being asked to use.

At this point, a thoughtful critic of the Pi Encryption will inevitably observe that, as the seven numbers with which we have to deal (386, 888, 100,000,000, 103,227,186, 120,390,965, 123,004,065 and

17766771) are not (in that critic's mind) related to each other in any meaningful way (in exactly the same way as if they had been picked at random out of a hat), the task we are setting ourselves is simply impossible to achieve.

But we shall soon see whether or not that really is the case – or whether, in the wonderful world of the Pi Encryption, we do in fact see **the impossible made possible before our very eyes.**

3. The "impossible" task – a brief summary

(1) find two mathematical courses to **17766771** (the key to the Pi Encryption);

(2) one must start with **386** ("Jesus" in Hebrew) and the other with **888** ("Jesus" in Greek);

(3) both must have exactly the same number of mathematical steps;

(4) each step must be identical, or very similar, to its corresponding step in the other course;

(5) apart from **386** and **888**, each course can only make use of the four Key Points, 10 and 1,000;

(6) only the simplest of mathematical "tools" (addition, subtraction, multiplication and division) may be used; and

(7) the calculation must be exact, with pinpoint precision to within one digit.

4. The "386" course to 17766771

The first part of the task before us is to plot an *exact* mathematical course, with *pinpoint precision*, from 386 to 17766771, using only 386 itself, the 4 Key Points, 10 and 1,000.

Let's see how we get on:

STEP ONE

We start with 386, by dividing it into Key Point A:

$$\frac{100{,}000{,}000}{386} = 259{,}067.3575$$

STEP TWO

Add the result of Step One to Key Points B, C and D:

259,067.3575	Result of Step One
103,227,186.0000	Key Point B
120,390,965.0000	Key Point C
123,004,065.0000	Key Point D
346,881,283.3575	

So far, we have used only 386 and each of the four Key Points.

STEP THREE

Divide the result of Step Two by the sum of Key Points A, B, C and D (446,622,216).

$$\frac{346{,}881{,}283.3575}{446{,}622{,}216} = 0.\mathbf{7766771}{\scriptstyle 80244656}$$

Already, after only 3 steps, we have arrived at a number (0.7766771) which contains, in the correct order, no fewer than 7 of the 8 digits of 17766771. But, striking though this is, we have not finished yet, because the task we have set ourselves is to find *all 8* of them.

STEP FOUR

Calculate the length of the Encryption Zone by subtracting Key Point A (100,000,000) from Key Point D (123,004,065):

	123,004,065	
-	100,000,000	
	23,004,065	- the length of the Encryption Zone

STEP FIVE

Multiply the result of Step Three by the result of Step Four:

0.776677180244656 x 23,004,065 = 17,866,732.33836478

STEP SIX

Divide 386 by 10:

386 ÷ 10 = 38.6

STEP SEVEN

Divide Key Point A (100,000,000) by 1,000:

100,000,000 ÷ 1,000 = 100,000

STEP EIGHT

Add the results of Steps Five and Six together:

17,866,732.33836478 + 38.6 = 17,866,770.93836478

STEP NINE

Subtract the result of Step Seven (100,000) from the result of Step Eight:

	17,866,770.9383
-	100,000.0000
	17766771 the Key to the Pi Encryption!

(see note 1)

And so we see how, in 9 simple steps, using only the simplest mathematical tools of addition, subtraction, multiplication and division, and working only with 386 itself, the 4 Key Points, 10 and 1,000, we can plot an *exact* course from 386 to 17766771.

I would challenge anyone to plot a similar course to 17766771, in 9 similar steps, using, instead of 386 and the 4 Key Points, five other, *randomly selected,* numbers.

I strongly suspect that one could spend a lifetime looking for a similar pattern devised from five *randomly selected* numbers, and still be unsuccessful.

And yet we can clearly see that "our" six numbers (386, 100,000,000, 103,227,186, 120,390,965, 123,004,065 and 17766771), assisted only by 10 and 1,000, fit together perfectly, effortlessly and seamlessly, exactly as one would expect them to do if they had been machine parts designed by a master engineer.

But the real significance of all this comes, not just from the pattern itself, but also from the astonishing fact that it is almost exactly mirrored by its companion course, based on 888, which follows in the next section – yes, the two of them can clearly be seen to reflect each other, step by step, with uncanny and undeniable clarity.

5. The "888" course to 17766771

As in the last section, the task we have been set is to plot an *exact* mathematical course to 17766771, only this time starting with 888, and using only 888 itself, the 4 Key Points, 10 and 1,000.

And again, just as before, we can only use the simplest mathematical "tools" of addition, subtraction, multiplication and division.

STEP ONE

Divide Key Point A (100,000,000) by 888:

$$\frac{100{,}000{,}000}{888} = 112{,}612.612612$$

STEP TWO

Subtract the result of Step One from the sum of Key Points A, B, C and D (446,622,216):

$$446{,}622{,}216 - 112{,}612.612612 = \underline{446{,}509{,}603.38738}$$

STEP THREE

Divide the sum of Key Points B-D (346,622,216) by the result of Step Two:

$$\frac{346{,}622{,}216}{446{,}509{,}603.38738} = 0.776292857690856$$

STEP FOUR

Calculate the length of the Encryption Zone by subtracting Key Point A (100,000,000) from Key Point D (123,004,065):

```
   123,004,065
 - 100,000,000
 -------------
    23,004,065  - the length of the Encryption Zone
```

STEP FIVE

Multiply the result of Step Three by the result of Step Four:

0.776292857690856 x 23,004,065 = 17,857,891.3573562

STEP SIX

Multiply 888 by 10:

888 x 10 = 8880

STEP SEVEN

Divide Key Point A (100,000,000) by 1,000:
100,000,000 ÷ 1,000 = 100,000

STEP EIGHT

Add the results of Steps Five and Six together:

```
   17,857,891.3573562
 +      8,880.0000000
 --------------------
   17,866,771.3573562
```

STEP NINE

Subtract the result of Step Seven (100,000) from the result of Step Eight:

$$
\begin{array}{r}
17{,}866{,}771.3573 \\
-\quad 100{,}000.0000 \\
\hline
\underline{\mathbf{17766771}}
\end{array}
$$

the Key to the Pi Encryption!

(see note 2)

6. Conclusion

Let us remind ourselves that there is absolutely *no* intrinsic or rational mathematical connection between 17766771 and Key Points B, C and D, except that the latter *just happen* to be the decimal place-numbers of the first three occurrences, in π, of the former.

As we saw in chapter 20, there is no reason to expect their connection to go any further than that, *and every conceivable reason to expect it not to.*

As independent expressions of two completely different digital registers, or dimensions, of π (17766771 being digits forming part of π itself and Key Points B, C and D being the first three decimal place-numbers in π where they happen to be located), neither of them should bear any mathematical relationship with, have any influence on, or be in any way affected or impacted by the other – any more than one would expect the number of days in the month of July to relate in some way to the population of China.

How wonderful it is therefore to know that, by these two "**386**" and "**888**" courses, all four Key Points, mediated in the case of the "**386**" course *only* by **386** itself ("Jesus" in Hebrew) 10 and 1,000, and in the case of the "**888**" course *only* by **888** itself ("Jesus" in Greek), 10 and 1,000, can be co-ordinated, in two mutually-corresponding 9 step patterns, to meet together at **17766771**, in *complete* precision and with *pinpoint* accuracy[(3)].

The evidential value of these two rigorously exact companion courses lies in the astonishing extent to which each of them mirrors the other at each corresponding step of the way. This can best be appreciated by referring to the diagram opposite, but, in brief:

a) in each course there are 9 steps; of which
b) 6 are exactly identical; and
c) the other 3 are strikingly similar.

Here we see **386** on the one hand and **888** on the other, marching in tandem, step by step, in perfect agreement with each other (and aided only by the 4 Key Points, 10 and 1,000), so as to meet and intersect precisely at **17766771**, that "superlative palindrome" which, as we saw in chapter 10, is itself the quintessential expression of them both, and the very Key by which the secrets of the Pi Encryption can be revealed!

Can *anyone*, even the most sceptical among us, not clearly see in all this God's **DEEP AND WONDERFUL DESIGN?**

The two parallel courses charted from **386** ("Jesus" in Hebrew) and **888** ("Jesus" in Greek) to **17766771** (the Key to the Pi Encryption)

	Step 1	Step 2	Step 3	Step 4	Step 5	Step 6	Step 7	Step 8	Step 9	Result
The 386 Course	A / 386	Add the result of Step 1 to (B+C+D)	Divide the result of step 2 by (A+B+C+D)	D – A	Multiply the result of step 3 by the result of step 4	Divide 386 by 10	A / 1,000	Add the results of steps 5 and 6 together	Subtract the result of step seven from the result of step 8.	17766771
The 888 Course	A / 888	Deduct the result of Step 1 from (A+B+C+D)	Divide (B+C+D) by the result of step 2	D – A	Multiply the result of step 3 by the result of step 4	Multiply 888 by 10	A / 1,000	Add the results of steps 5 and 6 together	Subtract the result of step seven from the result of step 8.	17766771
	identical	very similar	very similar	identical	identical	very similar	identical	identical	identical	

A = Key Point A (100,000,000)

B = Key Point B (103,227,186)

C = Key Point C (120,390,965)

D = Key Point D (123,004,065)

Notes on chapter 24

(1) The final result is 17766770.9384, which, being only 0.0616 short of 17766771, is more than adequate to satisfy the definition of "pinpoint precision" (accuracy to within one digit) adopted in the glossary of terms. It is accurate to within one part in well over 288,000,000.

(2) The final result is 17766771.3573, which, being only 0.3573 above 17766771, is more than adequate to satisfy the definition of "pinpoint accuracy" (accuracy to within one digit) adopted in the glossary of terms. It is accurate to within one part in well over 49,000,000.

(3) In accordance with this book's central policy of always going out of its way to *hinder*, *hamper*, and *handicap* the case for the Pi Encryption, and to *boost*, *bolster* and *buttress* the case against it, both of the surpassingly wonderful patterns in this chapter will be counted as if they were only one – feature 37.

CHAPTER 25

A CREDIBLE EXPLANATION?

In a round-up of every *conceivable* theory to explain the existence of the Pi Encryption, the theory of pure chance is found to be the only *potentially* viable alternative to that of divine design.

No intelligent reader, having been made aware of it, will fail to seek an explanation for the existence of the Pi Encryption.

If another explanation exists than that of <u>divine design</u>, this author is at a loss to imagine what it could possibly be.

And I daresay you are, too.

Can we just agree, here and now, that it is the only <u>viable</u> hypothesis?

But, if you still don't agree, what alternative hypothesis can you offer?

Perhaps, one of these:

"No Cause"

This would mean that the Encryption appeared in a causative vacuum – which is impossible, and simply amounts to avoiding the issue.

"Alien design"

Aliens (presumably of the extra-terrestrial variety) designed Pi. But how could they, unless they themselves existed independently of it?

"Delusion"

This improbably implies that everyone who sees the patterns of the Pi Encryption has been caught up in a permanent mass hallucination, from which no recovery is possible.

"Satanic Deception"

This would implausibly require a belief, not only that Satan, at some stage in the past, had power to alter Pi, but also that, in doing so, he aimed to glorify the name of Jesus and advance God's Kingdom on Earth!

"Reverse Engineering"

This would imply that the Biblical authors somehow conspired together to invent the name "Jesus", in order to satisfy the pre-existing design constraints of the Pi Encryption – but how, 2,000 years ago, could they have had any knowledge of the relevant digits of π?[(1)]

"Human Deception or Error"

This theory would depend on the patterns being the product of human trickery or error. But anyone with a 10 digit calculator can easily check all of them for himself at any time.

"Apothenia"

The dictionary definition of apothenia(2) is: "*the tendency to perceive a connection or meaningful pattern between unrelated or random things*". Typical examples would be an unjustified belief in conspiracy theories, or imagining that (in its sub-type known as "Pareidolia") one "saw" the face of a religious personage in a bowl of breakfast cereal.
Yet we have clearly seen that the patterns of the Pi Encryption are an *objectively* demonstrable mathematical fact, not this author's purely *subjective* interpretation of random or ambiguous patterns.

"The Multiverse"

It is a well established and cogent argument in favour of the existence of God that the extreme fine-tuning of the *fundamental physical constants* (such as the speed of light in vacuum, the gravitational constant, the Plank constant, etc) is so acute that any deviation, even by the tiniest fraction, from any of their observed values, would have rendered life impossible. To counter this, secularists have posited the theory, (for which there is no empirical evidence) that our universe may be but one of a large number, even an infinity, of universes (a "Multiverse"), of which only a tiny minority, because of their unique and randomly selected combination of values, could potentially host life. Were Pi merely a fundamental *physical* constant, then logically the same argument (though obviously weak) could be offered as an explanation for the existence of the Pi Encryption – that, in an infinity of universes, each with a different value for Pi, such an encryption will inevitably be generated not just once, but an infinite number of times. However, as Pi is a *mathematical* constant (i.e it has a fixed numerical value but does not directly involve any physical measurement), it must be taken to be invariable in and across all potential universes, even to infinity. As the assumed variability of constants across a theoretical multiverse is a key element in the secular case against God, and Pi is by definition *multiversally* invariable, for this reason alone (as well as the unproved and deeply improbable existence of the multiverse itself), any invocation of such reasoning as an explanation for the Pi Encryption would be fundamentally flawed.

"No design, an origin in pure chance"

One would have to believe that all these complex, interlocking and mutually corroborating patterns appeared by pure chance, randomly, as if by a roll of the dice.

As all the above hypotheses, except perhaps the last one, are devoid of any semblance of credibility, the remaining chapters of this book will be devoted to exploring whether or not this last theory, ("no design, an origin in pure chance") could ever amount to a sufficient or satisfactory explanation.

Notes to chapter 25

(1) As late as 1957, Pi had only been calculated to 7,480 places, increasing to 100,265 places in 1961 and 500,000 in 1967. It was only in January 1987, when Professor Yasumasa Kanada and his associates at the University of Tokyo calculated π to 2^{27} (134,217,728) places, that the digits of the Encryption Zone (place-numbers 100,000,001 to 123,004,065 inclusive) first became known to humanity (source: "Pi: a Source Book", Berggren, Borwein and Borwein, 1997, 2nd edition, page 685).

(2) Merriam-Webster online dictionary.

CHAPTER 26

ENCRYPTION DENIERS

Those who will deny even the most obvious of facts.

I think I can cautiously hope that at least some of those patient readers who have carefully and attentively travelled with me this far, will agree (though perhaps reluctantly) that the **Pi Encryption** is real.

Whether one likes it or not, its existence is an *objectively demonstrable fact.*

However, I have no doubt that there will be many others to whom the **Encryption** will seem so strange, and its implications so deep and so far-reaching, that, even at this point, they will still insist on denying it.

One obvious way for them to try to discredit the **Pi Encryption** (if that were possible) would be to prove that there were major and significant errors or miscalculations in this book; but, as every effort has been made to avoid any such errors or miscalculations, I am reasonably confident that none (or at least none that could fairly be described as "major and significant"), will be found.(1)

Even if there were any such errors, they could only reflect badly on this author, and not on the **Encryption** itself – unless, of course, they were so extensive and fundamental as to undermine its whole foundation, and not just one isolated part of it.

And, as has been stressed many times, any faults of this author have been more than adequately compensated for by the very conservative way in which the data have been presented – always in such a way as to massively *understate* the case for the **Pi Encryption**, by subjecting it to huge statistical handicaps (see chapter 27).

This surely means that the only remaining bolt-hole in which the determined **Encryption denier** can take refuge will be to argue that these exact, intricate and mutually corroborating patterns all came into existence *randomly*, as the unintended products of *blind chance.*

And so I must meet this challenge head on, and show that it is simply illogical, and a denial of sound reason, to attribute the **Pi Encryption** to a random process, rather than to the work of an **Intelligent Designer**.

The next three chapters will deal, therefore, in a very non-technical way, (because, like most of my readers, I am neither a trained mathematician nor an expert statistician), with the implications of the law of probability, as it applies to the principal features of the **Pi Encryption**.

The choice for you, the reader, is to decide whether you believe that the **Pi Encryption** arose by *chance* or by *design* – and, if by design, who *was* its Designer?

<u>Note on chapter 26</u>

(1) I am certainly not so foolish as to believe that there are no errors in this book. However, if there are any, they are honest ones, and therefore just as likely to go against the case I am making, as for it.

CHAPTER 27

"STACKING THE ODDS"

How, in order to avoid any accusation of distortion or exaggeration, the probability that the Pi Encryption came into being by mere chance will be massively *over*-estimated, and the probability that it was created by deliberate design will be massively *under*-estimated.

As you have read through this book from one chapter to the next, you will have noticed that the various characteristics of the **Pi Encryption**, the individual pieces of evidence from which its existence may be deduced, have been referred to as "**features**", and that they have been given serial numbers.

The total number of listed **features** is 37[(1)].

It will be obvious to everyone, simply by the application of common sense, that some of the findings detailed in this book are more intrinsically "probable" than others - in other words, that they are relatively more easy to attribute to chance, rather than to design.

For example, the findings listed in chapter 7 ("scratching at the surface") might fairly be regarded, even when they are all taken together, as a relatively minor part of the supporting evidence for the **Pi Encryption** - simply because, though unlikely, they do not fall outside the bounds of reasonable coincidence, especially in the context of an infinite series of digits such as π; whereas Feature 17 ("The Golden Pathway", see chapter 11) is clearly a much stronger part of the case for the **Pi Encryption**, because it links, with pinpoint precision, all four of the **Key Points** in a mathematically robust combination.

For me to attempt to calculate the "relative probabilities" (in this sense) of all 37 **features** would be well beyond both the scope of this book, and my mathematical capabilities!

And I suspect that it would contribute very little to your reading enjoyment.

Instead, in the probability calculations contained in the next chapter, I have focused mainly on just four of the most prominent **features**.

As for the other 33 **features**, I will adopt an "ultra cautious" approach, by attaching to each of them, as a deliberately harsh brake on the theory of design which I am advancing, exactly the same *artificially high and inflated* degree of probability.

In other words, the fundamental policy of this book is to avoid any suspicion of exaggerating the case for design, by deliberately and demonstrably *understating*, or *handicapping* it, by a *huge* margin, at *every* point.

This will ensure that no-one, however hostile or dismissive he or she may feel towards it, will be able to justify rejecting the **Pi Encryption** by reference to any alleged personal bias, fault, or over-enthusiasm, on this author's part.

The *artificially high* (i.e. hugely *over*-estimated) probability I have decided to attach to 33 out of the 37 listed **features** is a one in ten (1:10) chance.

Remember, the <u>lower</u> the number on the right, the <u>weaker</u> the case for the **Pi Encryption**. Thus, a probability of 1:10 is 10 times higher (or *less* favourable to the **Pi Encryption**) than 1:100, a hundred times higher than 1:1,000, etc.

This means that although the *actual* probability of a given **feature** occurring by mere chance would often, if calculated accurately, be one chance in thousands, millions, billions, or even trillions, nevertheless that **feature** will, for the purposes of this book, be assigned an *artificially high, unrealistically and grossly overstated* probability of one chance in ten (1:10).

By adopting this approach, I am deliberately and brutally *handicapping* the **Pi Encryption** so as to "stack the odds" heavily against it by a cumulative factor of many trillions.

Indeed, by trillions of trillions.

Let us go on now to the next chapter, where the results of this monstrously unfair contest ("unfair", that is, to the case for the **Pi Encryption**) are set out for all to see.

Note on chapter 27:

(1) There is a concise summary of all the 37 listed features in Appendix 10.

CHAPTER 27

CHAPTER 28

"HOW LIKELY IS IT?"

An attempt to estimate how likely (or rather how immensely *unlikely*) it is that the 37 listed features of the **Pi Encryption** arose together by mere chance, and not by design.

1. Introduction

In this chapter, we are going to test how *probable* (1) it is that the *patterns* described in this book are really no more than the accidental product of blind, mindless chance.

The governing standard by which such a test must be conducted is that of absolute certainty, represented in this book by the number "1".

When considering a future event, the symbol "1" represents absolute certainty that it will happen.

For example, if I deliberately place a coin on a flat surface with its head side up, the chance that it will be found to show "heads" and not "tails" is absolutely certain - "1".

And the chance that it will be found to show "tails" and not "heads" is nil - "0".

But if I flip the coin in the air and let it fall randomly, there is certainty ("1") only that:

(1) either a "head" or a "tail" will be thrown; and
(2) the chance of either one of them occurring is absolutely equal.

In this case, the certainty ("1") is split between two halves, each of which is expressed as "0.5".

There is a 0.5 chance of a "head", and a 0.5 chance of a "tail".

So much for single future events, such as tossing a coin once.

But what if one wanted to calculate the probability of tossing 2 "heads" in a row?

In that case, as the chance of a first "heads" in the first toss is 0.5 and that of a second "heads" in the second toss is also 0.5, the probability of two "heads" following one after the other is 0.5 x 0.5, or 0.5^2, which is 0.25.

In other words, there is a $^{25}/_{100}$ chance, or one chance in 4, that any two consecutive tosses will produce two "heads" (or two "tails").

And similarly, the chance that 4 tosses will produce 4 "heads" (or "tails") in a row is 0.5^4, or 0.0625, or one chance in 16.

The likelihood of 10 "heads" (or "tails") in a row is 0.5^{10}, or 0.0009765625, or one chance in 1,024 - and so on.

In precisely the same way, we can work out, in broad terms, the cumulative probability that the 37 listed **features** of the **Pi Encryption** arose merely by chance, and not by design.

And that is what we shall now proceed to do.

2. The known probabilities

As you know, in this book I have attempted to calculate the probability of four of the more outstanding listed **features**.

These are **features** 9 ("The Golden Pathway")[(2)], 10 ("Strangely Linked")[(3)], 18 (the first "Echo" pattern)[(4)] and 19 (the second "Echo" pattern) [(5)]

Each of these probabilities was found, even by itself, to be so exceedingly small as to virtually disappear from sight.

The probability of each of them separately and individually was:

<u>Feature 9</u> "The Golden Pathway" (see chapter 11, notes 3 and 4):

0.00000000000000000000000000000000001
(one chance in one hundred billion trillion trillion)

<u>Feature 10</u> "Strangely Linked" (see chapter 12, note 4 and Appendix 6):

0.000000000000000000000000000000008
(one chance in 125 million trillion trillion).

<u>Feature 18</u> the first "Echo Pattern" (see chapter 20 and Appendix 7):

0.00000000000000000004082
(one chance in 24 million, 490 thousand trillion); and

<u>Feature 19</u> the second "Echo Pattern" (see chapter 20 and Appendix 8):

0.000000000000000000002268
(one chance in 440 million, 920 thousand trillion).

And the probability of all of them occurring cumulatively (i.e. how likely it is that such a group of four complex patterns should all occur together in the same place and at the same time, *randomly*, and merely *by chance*) is calculated by multiplying their four individual probabilities together (just as we did with the coins in section 1 above), which comes to:

0.000000000000000000000000000000000
000000000000000000000000000000000
000000000000000000000000000000000
0000007406

But, tiny as that probability is, **it only accounts for 4 out of the 37 listed features!** Including the other 33 features (at the *ridiculously high* and *super-inflated* probability ratio of one chance in ten (1:10) proposed in chapter 27, so that no one can accuse us of exaggerating), increases our final result to the staggering:

0.000000000000000000000000000000
000000000000000000000000000000
000000000000000000000000000000
000000000000000000000000000000
0000000000000000007406

This vanishingly remote possibility amounts to less than one chance in 1,350,200 trillion, trillion, trillion, trillion, trillion, trillion, trillion, trillion, trillion, trillion, trillion, (or one trillion multiplied by itself ten times over, then multiplied again by 1,350,200).

Just how "big" a chance is that?

In the next chapter we shall be looking at some light-hearted illustrations of just how *immensely unlikely*(6) it is that the **Pi Encryption** could ever have arisen by *blind chance*, rather than by *deliberate design.*

Notes on chapter 28:

(1) The beginning of the process is for everyone to assume (quite rightly, in the absence of any evidence to the contrary) that there are no patterns in π, or that any that do exist are meaningless and random. In the same way, in a criminal trial, the accused person is entitled to a "presumption of innocence" which can only be reversed, so as to result in a verdict of "guilty" being recorded against him, if the prosecution produces enough credible evidence to satisfy the jury of his guilt "beyond reasonable doubt". As the trial progresses, the evidence builds up, until, in a successful prosecution, it becomes so compelling that the jury members no longer have any reasonable doubt that the accused person is guilty of the offence with which he has been charged. The defendant must be given the benefit of any reasonable doubt that may remain. If the prosecution fails to produce sufficient credible evidence to satisfy this very high standard, the accused person must be acquitted (whether or not he actually committed the crime) and will walk away from Court a free man. Here, as in a trial, I have presented you with many pieces of evidence, none of which, taken by itself, would necessarily be sufficient to prove my case. However, taken together, their very large number, consistent theme, pinpoint accuracy and mutually corroborative tendencies, can surely leave no room for any doubt – reasonable or otherwise – as to the existence and divine origin of the **Pi Encryption**.

(2) see chapter 11;

(3) see chapter 12;

(4) see chapter 20, part 4;

(5) see chapter 20, part 5;

(6) Clearly, one can never *completely* eliminate the *possibility* that something like the **Pi Encryption** could have arisen purely by chance. However, we all know that an accumulation of several individually inconclusive elements may be sufficient to build up such a compelling case as to justify practical certainty – proof "beyond reasonable doubt" – of a given fact. For instance, if one came across a single coin on the floor with its head side up, it would be impossible to tell, from that fact alone, whether it had been tossed, dropped, or deliberately placed there. However, if there were 9 other coins with it, all with their head sides up too, one could say, with confidence, that the chance or probability of their having been deliberately placed or arranged there by an *intelligent agent* was 1,024 times greater than of their having been tossed or dropped there in a random manner (because 0.5^{10} is 0.0009765625, or one chance in 1,024 - see section 1 of this chapter). And if, in addition, all 10 coins were neatly arranged at regular intervals and in a straight line, one could say, with absolute certainty, that an *intelligent agent* really must have been at work, as orderly arrangements of that kind simply do not happen by themselves. Such hallmarks of design as order, consistency, symmetry, pinpoint

accuracy and balanced measure, when found (as they are within the **Encryption Zone**) in such copious abundance as to render the operation of blind chance a practical impossibility, must be recognised and acknowledged by every person of good sense and sound judgment for what they undoubtedly are - proof "beyond reasonable doubt" of the existence, and divine origin, of the **Pi Encryption**.

CHAPTER 29

ILLUSTRATING THE IMPLAUSIBLE

Some *light-hearted* illustrations of how *seriously* unlikely it is that the **Pi Encryption** could ever have arisen by chance.

1. Introduction

As we saw in chapter 28, the likelihood of the 37 listed **features** of the **Pi Encryption** having arisen *randomly and by blind chance* and therefore *without being deliberately designed*, can be reliably shown to be considerably less than one chance in 1,350,200 trillion, trillion, trillion, trillion, trillion, trillion, trillion, trillion, trillion, trillion, trillion (or one trillion multiplied by itself ten times over, then multiplied again by 1,350,200).

In this chapter, we shall consider some *light-hearted* comparisons to illustrate how *seriously* unlikely this really is.

2. The Doomsday Ant

The ant population of the whole Earth has been estimated at upwards of 20,000,000,000,000,000 (twenty thousand trillion) at any one time.

I have no idea whether that figure is correct, but as this is only meant to be a light-hearted chapter, let's not get too bogged down with details. We can surely agree that there are an awful lot of ants in the world, and that's all we really need to know!

Imagine someone tells you that there is one ant, somewhere on Earth, that you must find and neutralise, or the world will suddenly be swallowed up in a cosmic "black hole", and everything will be destroyed in a veritable Ant Apocalypse.

This special doomsday ant looks and behaves exactly like all the others, but is the only one that has been endowed with all the unique characteristics it needs to bring about the ultimate cataclysm.

And you only have one shot at finding it!

And no way, just by looking at it, to tell which one it is!

As ants inhabit the entire land surface of the globe (apart from the Arctic, Antarctica and a few remote islands) you will have to start by deciding in which of the approximately 195 countries in the world to start looking for it.

Then, having decided on your country, you will have to choose which locality within that country to focus on.

Then, which particular area within that locality.

And which particular ant's nest in that area.

And finally, which one of the thousands of ants, in that particular nest, you think may be your target.

Remember, you have only one chance of picking the right ant, and it looks and behaves just like all the others!

I think you will agree that your chance of correctly selecting the one single doomsday ant out of all the trillions to choose from, *unaided by any outward clues*, (i.e. randomly), would, for all practical purposes, be as good as zero.

What a hopeless task!

How could you ever save the world?

And yet, incredibly, your chance of achieving success in this impossible task would be well over:

a trillion x a trillion
x a trillion
x a trillion
x a trillion
x a trillion
x a trillion
x a trillion
x a trillion
x a trillion = $(1{,}000{,}000{,}000{,}000^{10})$

times *better* than it would be for the 37 listed **features** of the **Pi Encryption** to have all just fallen into place together *randomly* and by *blind chance*!

Happy hunting!

3. Children tossing coins

Imagine a school assembly of 400 children. Each child is given a coin and the head teacher instructs them, at a given signal, to toss their coins and write down the result - "heads" or "tails".

Everyone's normal expectation, based on life experience and common sense, would be that on each throw, roughly half would be "heads" and the other half "tails".

Any significant divergence from a roughly equal split, for example 160 heads and 240 tails (2) would be extremely rare, even freakish - a statistical anomaly which may occur once in a great many flips, but certainly a very uncommon event.

But who would ever believe it if all 400 children reported a "head", in one single toss? Or if they all reported a "tail"? Not a single different result - everyone *exactly* the same!

Such a result would be so bizarre, freakish, uncanny and outlandish, that no one would ever believe it.

They would automatically infer that there must have been a flaw in the process - perhaps the coins were fake two-headed ones, or all the children had conspired to falsify their results, or even that everyone concerned had been subjected to mass hypnosis - in other words, that the freak result had somehow been orchestrated by some sort of cheating or scam (i.e. a form of *design*) rather than simply being the product of *chance*.

And yet the chance of every single one of the 400 children tossing a "head", or all of them tossing a "tail"(3), is at least a million trillion times *better* than the chance of the 37 listed **features** of the **Pi Encryption** all happening together by *blind chance*!

4. A Grand Worldwide Lottery

At the time of writing this, the estimated human population of the Earth is somewhere in the region of 8 billion.

Imagine that the United Nations Organisation announced they would be organising a monthly "Grand Worldwide Lottery".

In order to be fair to everyone, no tickets would be sold, as that would disadvantage the poor.

Instead, the names of everyone alive in the world - 8 billion people - would be entered automatically, and the lucky winner's name would be selected by a completely *random* process.

There would be *one* super jackpot prize winner per month. Only *one* winner per month out of 8 billion people.

And imagine that, when the result of the first monthly draw was announced, incredibly, *you* were that *one* lucky winner!

Alone out of 8 billion people, *your* name had been drawn, and no-one else's!

But imagine your astonishment if the same thing happened when the second monthly draw was announced! You had won again!

And the third!

And the fourth!

And the fifth, sixth, seventh, eighth, ninth, and tenth!

On each of ten consecutive monthly Grand Worldwide Lottery draws, you had won the jackpot - you alone, out of 8 billion people!

Would *anyone* believe that such a thing was possible?

Wouldn't you come under the closest investigation, to see by what trickery you had "fixed" the results?

And yet, incredibly, such an unimaginably implausible series of 10 consecutive Grand Worldwide Lottery prizes all being won by the same person(4) is well over *a trillion trillion trillion* (i.e. one trillion^3) times *more* probable than it would be for the 37 listed **features** of the **Pi Encryption** to have all "*just happened*" together, by *blind chance*!

Good Luck!

5. The Ragged Rascal

A well-known English tongue-twister is: "round the rugged rock the ragged rascal ran".

This phrase is made up of 36 letters and 7 spaces (43 features in all), each one of which must be correctly selected and placed, in the right order, for the phrase to read as it should.

Let us suppose that you are given 27 cards, on 26 of which are written the 26 letters of the alphabet, the 27th being blank (to represent a space).

Now, shuffle the cards well and select one of them at random. There is a 1:27 chance that it will be an "r", to spell the first letter in the phrase, "round". If it is not an "r", your first attempt to form the tongue-twister randomly will have failed, and you must start all over again.

Let's say that, against all the odds, you successfully select an "r" out of the 27 cards you have been given.

You must now put that card back with the others, shuffle them again, and select another card randomly, in the hope that it is an "o", to form the second letter of "round".

The chance of your getting this far, and successfully selecting an "o" as your second letter, is 1:27^2, or 1:729, or one chance in 729. If, as is highly likely, you are unsuccessful, you must go back and start the whole laborious process all over again.

Following this painstaking procedure, you can only reasonably expect to succeed in completing the whole tongue-twister, by random selection, in an average of one out of well over 35 trillion, trillion, trillion, trillion, trillion (i.e. 27^{43}) attempts.

But your chance of doing so is well over a trillion, trillion, trillion, trillion, trillion, trillion (i.e. one trillion ^{6}) times *better* than that of the Pi Encryption having come into existence by mere luck.

6. Pick your Atom!

According to a reliable online source [5], there are estimated to be something like 133 trillion, trillion, trillion, trillion (or one trillion to the power of four, times 133) atoms in Planet Earth. That includes all the rock in the Himalayas, Alps, Rockies and Andes, the sand in the Sahara and Kalahari Deserts, and everything in between them, and the core, mantle and crust of the Earth – as well, of course, as our own bodies and all the animals, birds, fish, insects and reptiles, the forests and prairies, cities, towns and villages, aircraft, trains, cars and buses - in fact, absolutely everything!

But in order to assemble a number of atoms equivalent to the odds against the **Pi Encryption** having occurred randomly, you would need (on that estimate) all the atoms from well in excess of a trillion, trillion, trillion, trillion, trillion, trillion, trillion (i.e. one trillion^{7}) planets just like Earth!

Notes on chapter 29:

(1) The very conservatively estimated chance of all 37 listed features of the **Pi Encryption** having arisen randomly is one chance in 1,350,200 x trillion^{11} (see chapter 28). As the estimated ant population of the world is about 20,000 trillion, one's chance, in this illustration, of selecting the right ant would be about 1:20,000 trillion, which is more than a trillion^{10} times better than 1:1,350,200 x trillion^{11}. The estimated number of 20,000 trillion ants is taken from a 2022 study by scientists at Hong Kong University.

(2) The probability of a 160/240 split of heads to tails (or vice versa) is less than one chance in 77,000.

(3) The chance of 400 children all recording exactly the same result when they simultaneously toss their coins (i.e. 400 straight "heads" or 400 straight "tails") is 0.5 to the power of 400 (0.5^{400}), which works out at roughly one chance in one trillion to the power of 10; whereas the probability of the 37 listed **features** of the **Pi Encryption** all happening together by "blind chance" is no more than one chance in one trillion to the power 11, multiplied by 1,350,200 – substantially more than one million trillion times *less* likely to happen.

(4) The probability of a single individual winning 10 successive lottery draws of the kind described above is one chance in 8 billion to the power of 10 ($1{:}8{,}000{,}000{,}000^{10}$), which is roughly one chance in one trillion^8 x 1,073. Microscopically tiny as such a chance clearly is, it is still well over a trillion trillion trillion times *greater* than that of the 37 listed **features** of the **Pi Encryption** all happening together by *"blind chance"* (roughly one chance in one trillion^{11} x 1,350,200).

(5) The U.S. Department of Energy's Thomas Jefferson National Accelerator Faculty in Virginia (see: Education.jlab.org/qa/mathatom05.html).

CHAPTER 29

CHAPTER 30

THE DECISION - WHAT SHOULD WE MAKE OF ALL THIS?

This final chapter contains an invitation to every reader to accept the Gospel of Jesus Christ and receive the gift of Everlasting Life that He alone can offer.

If one accepts, as I believe one must, that the **Pi Encryption** is real, what does it tell us about our human condition?

Firstly, and above all else, it tells us that there really is a God, without Whom no such miraculous signs as those found in the **Pi Encryption** could possibly have come into existence.

Secondly, it tells us that the name **JESUS** is central to everything that exists, just as Pi, as a universal constant, is fundamental to everything around us.

We can clearly see that **JESUS** is, quite literally, the **WORD** ("Logos") spoken of in the first verses of Saint John's Gospel:

> "In the beginning was the **Word**, and the **Word** was with **God**, and the **Word** was **God**. The same was in the beginning with **God**.

> All things were made by him; and without him was not any thing made that was made. In him was life; and the life was the light of men."

All mankind longs for this light but, tragically, so many of us - the vast majority - never seem to find it.

We search for it everywhere but in the only place where it can be found.

Until we find it, we are truly lost.

We put our faith in the false gods and fruitless idols of this world, but will not look upon the One True Saviour, to put our faith in Him.

We take care to **insure** our houses and cars, our jewellery and all our other worldly possessions, but do nothing to **ensure** our eternal destiny, the salvation of our souls!

When the **Pi Encryption** is so plain and unimpeachable, how can we possibly imagine that the One of whom it so clearly speaks - **JESUS CHRIST** - is of no relevance to our lives?

Aren't we all human?

As human beings, are we not all guilty (yes, <u>all</u> of us!) of breaking God's law?

Is there one of us who has not, at some time or another, lied, lusted, been greedy, stolen something, used God's name in vain, been filled with envy, or been unjustly angry with someone else?

Is there a single one of us who, at every waking moment of this life, has loved God with *all* his heart, mind, soul and strength? Can any of us truly say that we have *never* put the things of this world before our love of God?

This God of ours (the *only* One there is) is infinitely pure and holy and will judge us all, one day, according to His impossibly high standards of holiness - standards that only one person in history - **JESUS CHRIST** – has ever perfectly fulfilled.

To qualify for Heaven in our <u>own</u> strength (because of our <u>own</u> goodness, our <u>own</u> virtues and our <u>own</u> righteousness) we would have to achieve the same perfect score in the celestial holiness test as Jesus – 100 out of 100. Nothing less than that would do!

As it is written in scripture, (speaking of Heaven):

> "And there shall in no wise enter into it any thing that defileth, neither whatsoever worketh abomination, or maketh a lie; but they which are written in the Lamb's book of life".
>
> (Revelation, 21:27)

Being both *perfect* God and *perfect* Man, the Lord Jesus Christ - and He alone among all - could satisfy God's *perfect* standard - and provide the *perfect* atonement for our sins by His self-giving sacrifice on the cross at Calvary.

Do you not see how crucial this is for *all* of us, *without exception*?

> "And as it is appointed unto men once to die, but after this the judgment: So Christ was offered to bear the sins of many; and unto them that look for him shall he appear the second time unto salvation".
>
> (Hebrews 9.27,28)

Does not the *hard evidence* for Christianity presented, even in this little book, exceed by a thousandfold anything you have ever encountered in support of any other religion, faith-system or philosophy?

Does your present world-view offer you a Saviour, like Jesus, who is *truly* able to rescue you from your own sin?

Do you not owe it to yourself, *to your own immortal soul*, to say "yes" to Jesus?

The promise of Jesus is that, for all who *truly* believe in Him, He will write their names in His Book of Life, giving them new spiritual birth as citizens of His Heavenly Kingdom and members of His mystical Bride, the Church:

> "Him that cometh to me I will in no wise cast out ... And this is the will of him that sent me, that

> everyone which seeth the Son, and believeth on him, may have everlasting life: and I will raise him up at the last day".
>
> (John 6:37- 40).

The **Pi Encryption** is a standing, undeniable, unshakeable, testable, ever-present and enduring testimony to the truth of Christ's claims concerning His deity and the salvation that He *alone* can freely give to every soul who will trust in Him.

Because of his unique position as God's Son, **JESUS**, and **JESUS** alone, is able to rescue us from the eternal penalty due to us for our sins:

> "For God so loved the world, that he gave his only begotten Son, that whosoever believeth in him should not perish, but have everlasting life".
>
> (John 3.16)

> "Neither is there salvation in any other: for there is none other name under heaven given among men, whereby we must be saved".
>
> (Acts 4:12)

My plea to you, dear reader, is to take these eternal truths to heart and to reflect upon them in your innermost being:

- Can you *with integrity* reject or deny them?
- Can you *pretend* you never heard them?
- Can you *risk* dying in your sins?

There is a prayer you can pray, right now, if you will only humble yourself before God and accept His offer of salvation.

It is set out below.

> A prayer for salvation:
>
> "Lord Jesus Christ, I see now that you really are the Way, the Truth and the Life, the Only Son of God, the Redeemer of Mankind. I confess that I have sinned in thought, word and deed, and that I have no hope of Salvation except through You. I turn now from all my sinful ways to You alone, as my personal Lord and Saviour. According to Your promise, cleanse me now by Your precious blood, which You shed for me and for all sinners on the cross at Calvary. Give me new spiritual birth, write my Name in Your book of life, and fill me with your Holy Spirit, so that with Your help I may live according to Your Holy Will, and in obedience to Your Holy commandments, all the days of my life - Thank You, Lord Jesus. Thank You.
>
> Amen".

And what now?

If you have truly and sincerely prayed the prayer for salvation, you have put your faith in the Lord Jesus Christ alone, as your personal Saviour, and in doing so have taken an important first step, as a new Christian, in your lifelong pilgrimage of faith.

But to complete the journey and finally inherit everlasting life:

REPENT of your sins (which is a lifelong process);

BELIEVE in the Gospel (God will help you);

RECEIVE the Holy Spirit (in baptism); and

REMAIN in Christ (by obeying His word).

May God richly bless you, and keep you, and welcome you, at last, into His Eternal Kingdom,

In Jesus' Name,

Amen.

APPENDIX 1

The numerical values of the letters of the Hebrew alphabet

Usual form	Final form*	Name of letter**	Numerical value
א		Alef	1
ב		Bet	2
ג		Gimel	3
ד		Dalet	4
ה		He	5
ו		Vav	6
ז		Zayin	7
ח		Chet	8
ט		Tet	9
י		Yod	10
כ	ך	Kaf	20
ל		Lamed	30
מ	ם	Mem	40
נ	ן	Nun	50
ס		Samech	60
ע		Ayin	70
פ	ף	Peh	80
צ	ץ	Tsadeh	90
ק		Qof	100
ר		Resh	200
ש		Shin	300
ת		Tav	400

* Only used when the letter is at the end of a word, as the Mem is in "Elohim" (see Appendix 5).

** The English spelling of the names of Hebrew letters seems to vary quite significantly. For the purposes of this chart, the spelling used in the website of the Jewish Museum of London has been adopted.

APPENDIX 2

The numerical values of the letters of the Greek Alphabet (note 1)

Upper case form	Lower case form	Name of letter	Numerical value
Α	α	Alpha	1
Β	β	Beta	2
Γ	γ	Gamma	3
Δ	δ	Delta	4
Ε	ε	Epsilon	5
Ζ	ζ	Zeta	7
Η	η	Eta	8
Θ	θ	Theta	9
Ι	ι	Iota	10
Κ	ϰ	Kappa	20
Λ	λ	Lambda	30
Μ	μ	Mu	40
Ν	ν	Nu	50
Ξ	ξ	Xi	60
Ο	ο	Omicron	70
Π	π	Pi	80
Ρ	ϱ	Rho	100
Σ	σ or ς (note 2)	Sigma	200
Τ	τ	Tau	300
Υ	υ	Upsilon	400
Φ	φ	Phi	500
Χ	χ	Chi	600
Ψ	ψ	Psi	700
Ω	ω	Omega	800

(1) the obsolete letters digamma or vau (6), koppa (90) and sampi (900) have been omitted from this chart;

(2) the form "ς" is used when sigma appears at the end of a word, as it does in "Jesus" (Ι η σ ο υ ς) – see Appendix 4.

APPENDIX 3

"386"

<u>The numerical value of the letters of the name "Jesus" in Hebrew.</u>

The name "Jesus" in Hebrew is "Yeshua", which is written in Hebrew, from right to left, as follows:

י ש ו צ

(Please remember that, unlike Greek and English, Hebrew is a consonantal language, which means, for instance, that the vowel "e", which appears in the English spelling of "Yeshua", is not represented in the Hebrew).

	<u>letter</u>	<u>numerical value</u>
the "Y" is expressed by a Yod:	י	10
the "sh" by a Shin:	ש	300
the "u" by a Vav:	ו	6
and the "a" by an Ayin:	צ	<u>70</u> <u>386</u>

The numerical value of the letters of the name "Jesus" in Hebrew is therefore **<u>386</u>**

APPENDIX 4

"888"

<u>The numerical value of the letters of the name "Jesus" in Greek.</u>

The name "Jesus" in Greek is "Iesous" (I η σ ο υ ς).

	letter	numerical value
the letter "I" is expressed by an iota:	I	10
the "e" by an eta:	η	8
the first "s" by a sigma:	σ	200
the "o" by an omicron:	ο	70
the "u" by an upsilon:	υ	400
and the final "s" by a sigma (final form – see Appendix 2, note 2):	ς	200
		888

The numerical value of the letters of the name "Jesus" in Greek is therefore **888**

APPENDIX 5

"86"

The numerical value of the letters of the word "God" in Hebrew.

The first name* used for "God" in the Bible is "Elohim", which is written in Hebrew, from right to left, as follows:

אלהימ

(Please remember that, unlike Greek and English, Hebrew is a consonontal language, which means, for instance, that the vowel "o", which appears in the English spelling of "Elohim", is not represented in the Hebrew).

	letter	numerical value
the "E" is expressed by an Alef:	א	1
the "l" by a Lamed:	ל	30
the "h" by a He:	ה	5
the "i" by a Yod:	י	10
and the "m" by a Mem (final form):	ם	40
		86

The numerical value of the letters of the Hebrew name for God, "Elohim", is therefore 86

* It appears in the very first verse of the Bible, Genesis 1:1.

APPENDIX 6

(see chapter 12)

Calculation of how probable it is that any three four-digit combinations (none of which starts with "0") will, if selected at random, all contain the digits 0, 1, 2 and 3

(1) Take any set of 4 different digits (such as 0, 1, 2 and 3), and you will find that there are just 24 different ordinal combinations into which the set can be sorted.

(2) In the case of the particular set are we are studying, 0, 1, 2 and 3 ("the Study Set") they are these:

0123	0132	0213	0231	0312	0321
1023	1032	1203	1230	1302	1320
2013	2031	2103	2130	2301	2310
3012	3021	3102	3120	3201	3210

(3) As no whole number can start with a zero, and place numbers in π can only be whole numbers, we must discount from this calculation the 6 combinations in paragraph 2 that start with a zero, leaving 18 of the original 24.

(4) There are therefore 18 different combinations of the Study Set that are capable of forming the first four digits of a decimal place number in π.

(5) Our aim is to find out how probable it is that any three 4 digit combinations (none of which starts with a "0"), *if they are selected at random*, will all be different combinations of the Study Set.

(6) The range of possible 4 digit combinations from which the selection must be made is from 1000 to 9999 inclusive – a total of 9,000 combinations. (N.B. the first 1,000

combinations, from 0000 to 0999 inclusive, must be discounted for the purposes of this calculation, for the reason already explained in paragraph 3).

(7) As there are 18 different ordinal combinations of the Study Set that are capable of forming the first 4 digits of a place number in Pi (such as Key Points B, C and D), and 9,000 possible combinations from which they can be selected, it follows that the chance of any randomly selected group of 4 digits being one of the 18 is:

$$\frac{18}{9{,}000} = 0.002$$

(8) It also follows that the cumulative probability of 3 simultaneously and randomly selected groups of 4 digits all happening, by blind chance, to belong to the 18 is just:

0.002^3

<u>or:</u> 0.000000008

<u>or:</u> **<u>one chance in one hundred and twenty-five million.</u>**

APPENDIX 7

(see chapter 20)

Calculation of how probable it is that any two 8 digit sections of π will, *if selected at random*: (A) both be the same (such as, for instance, 17766771); and (B) be separated from each other by a number of decimal places in π (such as 19,776,871) of which 5 of its 8 digits match their ordinal counterparts in the two identical 8 digit sections of π that were randomly selected.

(A) "Will both be the same (such as, for instance, 17766771)"

As we saw in chapter 5, note 2, all sequences of 8 digits (such as 17766771) are generally distributed, in Pi, so as to occur, on average, once in every 100,000,000 decimal places. It follows that the likelihood of any two *randomly selected* 8 digit sequences in Pi both being the same (e.g. both being 17766771) is 1:100,000,000^2, or *one chance in ten thousand trillion.*

(B) "Will be separated from each other by a number of decimal places in π (such as 19,776,871) of which 5 of its 8 digits match their ordinal counterparts in the two identical 8 digit sections of π that were randomly selected"

(1) The two sequences under consideration are:

17766771

and: 19776871

(2) As there are 10 digits (0-9 inclusive) to select from, if the two sequences were selected *randomly*, the chance of

any digit in one of the sequences matching its ordinal counterpart in the other sequence would be one chance in 10, or 0.1, thus:

1	(match)	**1**	x 0.1
7	(no match)	**9**	-
7	(match)	**7**	x 0.1
6	(no match)	**7**	-
6	(match)	**6**	x 0.1
7	(no match)	**8**	-
7	(match)	**7**	x 0.1
1	(match)	**1**	x 0.1

(8 attempts, resulting in 5 matches and 3 mismatches)[(1)] [(2)]

(3) The overall probability of these two sequences (17766771 and 19776871) being generated by pure chance is 0.00040824, or one chance in 2,449 (calculated, using a binomial calculator, as being the probability of achieving 5 successes in 8 attempts, where, as above, the probability of each of the attempts succeeding is 0.1)

(C) Cumulative Probability

The probability of the outcomes at (A) and (B) both occurring together, by blind chance, in one *randomly generated* **pattern** is therefore:

The probability of (A) x the probability of (B)

or 1: ($100{,}000{,}000^2$ x 2,449)
or one chance in:
24 million, 490 thousand, trillion.

<u>**Notes on Appendix 7**</u>

(1) For the sake of simplicity, I have deliberately omitted from this calculation any consideration of the fact that, as the first digit in the right-hand column cannot be a zero (because the right-hand column can only contain a whole number), the chance of a match in that line is actually 1:9, or 0.111' <u>not</u> 0.10. However, somewhat counter-intuitively, the effect of this deliberate omission is actually to *weaken* the case I am advancing, not strengthen it, because it reduces the number of attempts for use in the necessary binomial calculation from 8 to 7, resulting in an overall probability of 1:3,532 (i.e. 0.00255 x 0.111), rather than 1:2,449.

(2) Another way in which this calculation errs to the detriment of the case I am advancing is that it assumes (against the odds) that the number of decimal places for use in the right-hand column will always have eight digits, making a comparison of this kind possible. The reality is, however, that in many cases it will not.

APPENDIX 8

(see chapter 20)

Calculation of how probable it is that any two 8 digit sections of π will, *if selected at random*: (A) both be the same (such as, for instance, 17766771); and (B) be separated from each other by a number of decimal places in π (such as 17,163,771) of which 6 of its 8 digits match their ordinal counterparts in the two identical 8 digit sections of π that were randomly selected.

(A) "Will both be the same (such as, for instance, 17766771)"

As we saw in chapter 5, note 2, all sequences of 8 digits (such as 17766771) are generally distributed, in π, so as to occur, on *average*, once in every 100,000,000 decimal places. It follows that the likelihood of any two *randomly selected* 8 digit sequences in π both being the same (e.g. both being 17766771) is 1:100,000,000^2, or *one chance in ten thousand trillion.*

(B) "Will be separated from each other by a number of decimal places in Pi (such as 17,163,771) of which 6 of its 8 digits match their ordinal counterparts in the two identical 8 digit sections of π that were randomly selected."

(1) The two sequences under consideration are:

17766771

and: 17163771

(2) As there are 10 digits (0-9 inclusive) to select from, if the two sequences were selected *randomly*, the chance of any digit in one sequence matching its ordinal counterpart in the other sequence would be one chance in 10, or 0.1, thus:

1	(match)	**1**	x 0.1
7	(match)	**7**	x 0.1
7	(no match)	**1**	-
6	(match)	**6**	x 0.1
6	(no match)	**3**	-
7	(match)	**7**	x 0.1
7	(match)	**7**	x 0.1
1	(match)	**1**	x 0.1

(8 attempts, resulting in 6 matches and 2 mismatches)(1) (2)

(3) The overall probability of these two sequences (17766771 and 17163771) being generated by pure chance is 0.00002268, or one chance in 44,092 (calculated, using a binomial calculator, as being the probability of achieving 6 successes in 8 attempts, where, as above, the probability of each of the attempts succeeding is 0.1)

(C) Cumulative Probability

The probability of the outcomes at (A) and (B) both occurring together, by blind chance, in one *randomly generated* **pattern** is therefore:

The probability of (A) x the probability of (B)

or 1:($100,000,000^2$ x 44,092)
or one chance in:
440 million, 920 thousand, trillion.

Notes on Appendix 8

(1) see note (1) on Appendix 7, which also applies here;

(2) see note (2) on Appendix 7, which also applies here.

APPENDIX 9

(see chapter 20, note 5)

Calculation of how probable it is that *both* the "echo" patterns described in chapter 20 came about together, randomly and *by pure chance* – (i.e. without being designed).

(A) As we saw in Appendix 7, the probability of the first "echo" pattern described in chapter 20 arising randomly can be reliably calculated at:

$$1:100{,}000{,}000^2 \times 2{,}449$$

or one chance in

24 million, 490 thousand, trillion.

(B) As we saw in Appendix 8, the probability of the second "echo" pattern described in chapter 20 arising randomly can be reliably calculated at:

$$1:100{,}000{,}000^2 \times 44{,}092$$

or one chance in

490 million, 920 thousand, trillion.

(C) It follows therefore that the cumulative probability of both the "echo" patterns arising together randomly and purely by chance, can be reliably calculated at:

$$1: (100{,}000{,}000^2 \times 100{,}000{,}000^2 \times 2{,}449 \times 44{,}092)$$

or $1: (100{,}000{,}000^4 \times 107{,}981{,}308)$

or $1: (107{,}981{,}308 \times 10^{32})$

or one chance in well over: **10,798 trillion, trillion, trillion**

APPENDIX 10

A concise summary of the 37 features of the **Pi Encryption** listed in this book.

Feature Number	Where Discussed	Concise Summary
1	Chapter 5	1. The first 3 occurrences in π of the digit-string **17766771** (the key to the **Pi Encryption**) all occur, in a close-knit and unlikely cluster, within a section of π which is less than 20,000,000 decimal places in length; 2. Although the probability of a cluster of **17766771's** such as this occurring anywhere in π is quite low, this particular one occurs so near to the beginning of π that it is relatively easy for us to identify; and 3. The distance between the first and the third occurrences of **17766771** is 19776879 decimal places, incorporating **1776** (or twice **888** – "Jesus") within it. Furthermore, one half of 19776879 is 9888439.5.
2	Chapter 7	1. The distance between **Key Points A** and **C** when expressed as a fraction of the overall length of the **Encryption Zone**, is 0.886 (888 = "Jesus" in Greek); 2. The overall length of the Encryption Zone, when multiplied by 0.386 ("Jesus" in Hebrew) produces 8880,000 ("Jesus" in Greek);

		3. The distance between Key Points B and D, when expressed as a fraction of the overall length of the Encryption Zone is 0.**86** ("God" in Hebrew); 4. The aggregate value of the digits of the decimal places of the first three occurrences in π of the key to the Pi Encryption (17766771) is **86** ("God" in Hebrew); 5. Key Point B (the first occurrence in π of the key to the Pi Encryption 17766771) ends with an "**86**" ("God" in Hebrew); and 6. Each of Key Points C and D (the second and third such occurrences) ends with "65" (which is the aggregate value of the digits in Key Points B and C).
3	Chapter 8	1. The distance of Key Point B from the start of the Encryption Zone, when inverted and halved, reveals **386** ("Jesus" in Hebrew); and 2. The distance between Key Points C and D (the second and third occurrences in π of the key to the Pi Encryption, (17766771), when inverted, produces **386** ("Jesus" in Hebrew).
4	Chapter 9	**614086** ("Jesus is God") exactly represents: (1) the number of decimal places by which the distance between **Key Point A** and **Key Point B,** exceeds

		that between **Key Point C** and **Key Point D;** (2) the difference between the length of the **First Section of the Encryption Zone** (17,777,865 decimal places) and the distance between **Key Points B and C** (17,163,779 decimal places); and (3) the difference between the position of **Key Point C** within the **Encryption Zone** (20,390,965) and the number of decimal places between **Key Points B** and **D** (19,776,879).
5	Chapter 10	The key to the **Pi Encryption** (<u>**17766771**</u>) is a *double* palindrome, in that two separate but overlapping elements, each conveying its own intrinsic message (<u>**1776**</u> - "Jesus" x 2 in Greek and 771 – "Jesus" x 2 in Hebrew) are *both* palindromised.
6	Chapter 10	The key to the **Pi Encryption** (<u>**17766771**</u>) is a fully reciprocating palindrome, in that the two elements start on opposite sides and cross over, 1776 on the left answered by 6771 on the right, and 771 on the right answered by 177 on the left.
7	Chapter 10	The two elements of the "superlative palindrome" (<u>**17766771**</u> – the key to the **Pi Encryption**) both conform to a common scheme, or pattern, in that one (<u>**1776**</u>) is *double* the name of Jesus in Greek (<u>**888**</u>), and the other (771) is as close to *double* the name of Jesus in

		Hebrew (**<u>386</u>**) as is possible to have, in order to form a perfect palindrome.
8	Chapter 10	The two elements of the "Superlative Palindrome" (**<u>17766771</u>**, the key to the **Pi Encryption**) have identical *meanings* in Hebrew and Greek – none other than twice the name of Jesus (**<u>386</u>** and **<u>888</u>**).
9	Chapter 11	There is a six-step "Golden Pathway" linking all four of the **Key Points** together, with pinpoint accuracy: (1) subtract **Key Point A** from each of **Key Points C** and **D**; (2) take the last 6 digits of **Key Point B**, and convert them into a decimal fraction; (3) halve the result; (4) invert that result; and (5) multiply **Key Point D** (as reduced by **Key Point A** – see step one) by the result of (4), producing a final result which is exactly (to within one decimal place) the reduced form of **Key Point C**! It can be seen from this that all 4 Key Points are placed in a precise relationship with each other, such that if the position of any one of them had been even slightly different, this pattern would not have existed.
10	Chapter 12	The first 4 digits of the decimal place numbers of each of the first three occurrences, in π, of the key to the **Pi Encryption** (<u>17766771</u>) are all either 0, 1, 2 or 3. The combined odds *against* such a "strange linkage" occurring randomly, or by pure chance, are huge.

11	Chapter 13	The sum (346,622,216) of the decimal place numbers of the first three occurrences, in π, of the key to the **Pi Encryption** (**<u>17766771</u>**), when multiplied by 4, produces a 10 digit number which includes both **<u>386</u>** ("Jesus" in Hebrew) and **<u>888</u>** ("Jesus" in Greek).
12	Chapter 15	The distances separating the first three occurrences, in π, of the key to the **Pi Encryption** (**<u>17766771</u>**), when multiplied together, produce **<u>888</u>** ("Jesus" in Greek).
13	Chapter 16	By adding the decimal place numbers of the first and third occurrences, in π, of the key to the **Pi Encryption** (**<u>17766771</u>**), then inverting and halving the result, we find **<u>386</u>** ("Jesus" in Hebrew) embedded at the core.
14	Chapter 16	By adding the decimal place numbers of the first and second occurrences, in π, of the key to the **Pi Encryption** (**<u>17766771</u>**), then halving and inverting the result, we find **<u>888</u>** ("Jesus" in Greek) embedded at the core.
15	Chapter 17	How the decimal place numbers of all four **Key Points** can in three simple steps be connected with a sequence containing both **<u>1776</u>** ["**<u>888</u>**" (Jesus in Greek) x 2] - and **<u>888</u>** ("Jesus" in Greek).

16	Chapter 18	The essential digital features (1776-771) of the "Superlative Palindrome" of Chapter 10 (<u>**17766771**</u>) are to be found deeply embedded in the first three occurrences, in π, of the key to the **Pi Encryption** (that same <u>**17766771**</u>) and can be revealed by a simple four-stage process of addition, multiplication and subtraction.
17	Chapter 19	The non-palindromised form (17766772) of the Key to the **Pi Encryption** (17766771) is found embedded within **Key Point B.**
18	Chapter 20	The number of decimal places (19,776,871) between the first and the third occurrences, in π, of the key to the **Pi Encryption** (<u>**17766771**</u>) differs from <u>**17766771**</u> itself by only three digits. The probability of this happening *randomly* is one chance in 2,449. When taken together with the other elements of this overall pattern, the probability of such a formation coming into existence randomly (i.e. without design) is microscopically small.
19	Chapter 20	The number of decimal places (17,163,771) between the first and the second occurrences, in π, of the key to the **Pi Encryption** (<u>**17766771**</u>), differs from <u>**17766771**</u> itself by only 2 digits. The probability of this happening

		randomly is only one chance in 44,092. When taken together with the other elements of this overall pattern, the probability of such a formation coming into existence randomly (i.e. without design) is microscopically small.
20	Chapter 20	By lining up, one above the other, the numbers of decimal places between the first and the third and the first and the second occurrences, in π, of the key to the **Pi Encryption** (**17766771**), and systematically selecting alternate digits from each of them in an orderly progression, the key to the **Pi Encryption (17766771)** is exactly reproduced.
21	Chapter 20	By lining up, one above the other, the numbers of decimal places between the first and the third and the first and the second occurrences, in π, of the key to the **Pi Encryption** (**17766771**), and systematically eliminating the digits in each line that do not correspond to their ordinal counterparts in **(17766771)**, we find, against extremely long odds, that every single vertical column contains at least one (and, in three cases, two) corresponding digits.

22	Chapter 22	The "**essential components**" 2614386 and 17777865 with Key Points A, C and D, can be combined together, in seven steps, to produce 1776666771 – the First Pathway.
23	Chapter 22	The "**essential components**" 2614386 and 17777865 with Key Points A, B and D, can be combined together, in eight steps, to produce 17766772 – the Second Pathway.
24	Chapter 22	The "**essential components**" 2614386, 17777865, 386 and 17766888, with Key Point A, can be combined together, in nine steps, to produce 17766888 – the Third Pathway.
25	Chapter 22	The "**essential component**" 2614386 can be combined with Key Points A, B, C and D in seven steps, to produce 17766772 – the Fourth Pathway.
26	Chapter 22	The "**essential component**" 2614386 can be combined with Key Points A, B and D, in six steps, to produce 17766888 – the Fifth Pathway.
27	Chapter 22	The "**essential component**" 2614386 can be combined with Key Points A, B and D, in six steps, to produce 446,622,216 (i.e. A + B + C + D) – the Sixth Pathway.

28	Chapter 22	The "**essential component**" 2614386 can be combined with 386, 17766772, 17777865 and Key Point A, in nine steps, to produce 17766772 – the Seventh Pathway.
29	Chapter 22	The "**essential components**" 2614386, 386, 17766772 and Key Point A can be combined together, in six steps, to produce 17766772 – the Eighth Pathway.
30	Chapter 22	The "**essential components**" 2614386, 386, 17766888 and Key Point A can be combined together, in six steps, to produce 17766888 – the Ninth Pathway.
31	Chapter 22	The "**essential components**" 2614386 and 17777865, with Key Points A, C and D, can be combined together, in nine steps, to produce 1776666772 – the Tenth Pathway.
32	Chapter 22	The "**essential components**" 2614386, 17777865 and Key Points A, B and D, can be combined together, in ten steps, to produce 17766772 – the Eleventh Pathway.
33	Chapter 22	The "**essential components**" 2614386, 17777865, and Key Points A, B and D, can be combined together, in eight steps, to produce 17766888 – the Twelfth Pathway.

34	Chapter 22	The "**essential components**" 2614386, 17777865 and Key Points A, B, C and D, can be combined together, in nine steps, to produce 17766772 – the Thirteenth Pathway.
35	Chapter 22	The "**essential elements**" 2614386, 17777865, and Key Points A, B and D, can be combined together, in nine steps, to produce 446,622,216 (i.e. A + B + C + D) – the Fourteenth Pathway.
36	Chapter 23	A "**Heavenly Pathway**" can be charted between **386** ("Jesus") and **17766771** (the key to the Pi Encryption) in nine steps using only 386 itself, the 4 Key Points, 5, 10 and 100.
37	Chapter 24	An *exact* mathematical course can be charted from **386** ("Jesus") to **17766771** (the key to the Pi Encryption), in nine steps using only **386** itself, the 4 Key Points, 10 and 100; a similar nine-step course can also be charted from **888** ("Jesus") to **17766771** (the Key to the Pi Encryption), using only **888** itself, the four Key Points, 10 and 100; and what is more, the two courses correspond identically (or very similarly) at each step of the way.

APPENDIX 11

A VERY IMPORTANT QUESTION:

Is "Jesus" the *only* personal forename encrypted in π, and if so, how can we be sure?

1. This is a very important question indeed, because if "Jesus" were found *not* to be the only personal forename encrypted in π, this would tend to detract from, and to undermine, the unique honour and acclaim that are due *only* to Him. It would also strongly suggest that such a sublime mystery as the **Pi Encryption** could have somehow "just happened", by blind chance, in a higgledy-piggledy manner, as it is impossible to believe that any divine Designer of such an encryption would have contrived to hide the name of any *ordinary* person (like you or me) within it, on a par with that of the **Lord Jesus Christ!**

2. My short answer to the question asked above is:

   "Yes, we can be sure, *beyond all reasonable doubt,* that "Jesus" really is the only personal forename encrypted in Pi!"

   And we shall go on now to consider, in detail, my justification for making this bold assertion.

3. **The justification for this assertion**

   In order to prove my shamelessly bold assertion to be true (that we can be sure, *beyond all reasonable doubt*, that "Jesus" really is the only personal forename encrypted in π), we need to begin by asking how many human forenames there are, or have been, that could theoretically be found encrypted in **π.**

I have considered two possible ways to approach this question:

4. **Approach "A"**

As almost every human being in history has been given a name, the question of how many human forenames could potentially be encrypted in π, might (according to this approach) be answered by calculating how many human beings have been born since the first appearance of mankind on Planet Earth. However, there are three obvious weaknesses to this approach, namely that: (a) it assumes that every human being that has ever lived has had an individual forename different from everyone else, which of course is not the case; (b) it assumes that we can be sure how many human beings have ever lived, which of course we cannot; and (c) it assumes that all possible human forenames have already been used, which of course they have not.

5. **Approach "B"**

The other possible approach is simply to use, as the basis for one's calculation, the number of *theoretically possible* human forenames of between one and a suitably higher number of (say) twelve letters. This inevitably makes allowance for literally trillions of weird, bizarre, absurd and often totally unpronounceable potential 1-12 letter combinations, the like of which, one can be absolutely certain, has never actually been foisted upon any poor child (nor hopefully ever will be). Four extreme, but nevertheless pronounceable, twelve-letter humorous examples of this, would be "Dribblychops", "Humptydumpty", "Cantankerous" and "haemorrhoids", none of which is ever likely to be inflicted on any unfortunate infant – but there are also many billions of totally unpronounceable and fanciful examples, such as

"Zmkvbtcfhsqz" and "kkkkkkkkkkkk". According to this approach, the total number of potential 1-12 letter human forenames is just under one hundred thousand trillion (1).

6. **The basis of comparison**

Please note that, as we should only compare "like with like":

(a) we are only concerned here with *forenames* (because "Jesus" is a forename), and not with surnames, nicknames, titles or patronymics; and

(b) by "encryption", we mean a level of encryption that, in its complexity, pinpoint accuracy, internal cohesion and thematic consistency, is reasonably comparable with that which we have seen described in this book, *and nothing less.*

7. **The development of Approach "A"**

Approach "A" requires a calculation of the number of human beings who have been born since the human race first appeared on Planet Earth.

According to the calculations of The Population Reference Bureau(2), the total number of people who have ever lived on Earth is in the region of 108,000,000,000 (one hundred and eight billion).

Now, assuming that every one of those 108 billion people had a forename, we may be said to have a reasonable starting-point on which to base our calculations.

8. **A major objection to Approach "A"**

But, unfortunately, there may be some readers who will suspect that I am attempting to manipulate the figures, in order to give undeserved weight to the case for the **Pi Encryption**.

They may suggest that 108 billion is far too low a figure to use, as humanity (they may say) has been in existence for much longer than that number supposes.

Or they may suggest that the statisticians at The Population Reference Bureau (despite their expertise,[(2)]) have been far too conservative in their calculations (for instance, by not making a correct allowance for high rates of infant mortality in the past, or for the effects of warfare, plague and famine), and that because of this their figure of 108 billion is far too low and should therefore be disregarded.

9. I must be very vigilant to guard against any such suspicion of my methods or motives, as I honestly have no wish to mislead anyone (myself included) into believing something that isn't true – or even to give the *impression* that I wish to do so.

   In order to be seen to be fair to the doubters, and to avoid any suspicion of foul play, I am going to "load the dice" massively *against* the case I am making, by skewing the figures in such a way as to subject the case for the **Pi Encryption** to **a huge practical handicap.**

10. **Here's how:**

    (1) I shall *totally* ignore the obvious and important fact that hardly anyone has a completely unique forename, and that almost everybody shares his or her name with hundreds, thousands or even millions of other people (just think how many people there are in the world named John, Maria, Ibrahim or Fatima, to name but four, and you will see what a huge difference this makes); and

    (2) I shall multiply the already enormous figure of 108 billion that we considered above, by a factor of one million

(1,000,000), so as to arrive at a purely arbitrary (but obviously hugely excessive) working total of **108 thousand trillion**. The effect of this is a *massive* and *totally unrealistic exaggeration* of the estimated number of human beings who have been born since mankind first appeared on Earth (and, with it, the number of actual or potential forenames we have to allow for in our calculations).

In each case my purpose, in introducing these fictions, is to *deliberately falsify* the figures, by a *huge* margin – not in favour, but *against* the case I am making – in order to distance myself from even the slightest suspicion of exaggeration.

11. **My "Confession":**

I hereby fully and frankly confess to falsifying these figures in a shameless, outrageous and shocking way – but only so as to massively *weaken* the case I am making, and give an enormous (but totally undeserved) boost - to the opposition!

12. **A merger of the two Approaches, A and B.**

As we saw above, our over-generous estimate of the number of actual or potential human forenames came to about 108 thousand trillion, when calculated according to Approach "A", and to just under 100,000 trillion, when calculated according to Approach "B". As these two figures are only about 8,000 trillion apart from each other, it seems reasonable to adopt the higher of the two for the purpose of our calculations, and, for the sake of simplicity, that is what we shall do.

13. It should not go without notice however that, by adopting the *higher* of the two figures, I am once again *handicapping* the case

for the **Pi Encryption**, in *favour* of that of its critics, by a further enormous margin - as it freely concedes, to the *opponents* of the **Pi Encryption**, an additional 8,000 trillion *more* potential human forenames (and therefore chances of succeeding), than they would otherwise have had.

14. **Methodology**

The best way to illustrate our methodology is to liken what we are doing to a lottery, in which the number of tickets sold is equivalent to the total (hugely exaggerated) number of actual, potential and notional human forenames we decided in paragraph 12 to use for this purpose (108 thousand trillion).

15. According to the rules of our "lottery", each of those actual, potential and notional 108 thousand trillion forenames (which *include* "Jesus") has an equal chance, when the lottery is drawn, of "winning the jackpot" (that is, of forming the centrepiece of a complex web of cryptic patterns comparable to the **Pi Encryption**).

16. Each of the actual, potential and notional 108 thousand trillion human forenames, with its unique combination of letters, will have to be rendered into Hebrew and Greek lettering, and then each set of Hebrew and Greek letters will have to be converted into their numerical equivalents, according to the tables in Appendices 1 and 2.

17. Once this process of converting the 108 thousand trillion forenames into their Hebrew and Greek numerical equivalent values has been completed, it will be seen that, just like the name "Jesus" (**386** in Hebrew and **888** in Greek), we have two numbers for each forename – the raw material for a potential *chance encryption* in π !

18. But, as we saw in chapter 28, the probability of a group of patterns such as the **Pi Encryption** (based on *any* two numbers, such as **386** and **888**, regardless of whether or not they are linked to any particular name) occurring by chance is estimated (with extreme generosity to critics of the Pi Encryption) at no higher than one chance in one trillion to the power of eleven, multiplied by 1,350,200 – in other words, one trillion multiplied by itself ten times over and then multiplied again by 1,350,200.

19. So how likely is it, then, that any of our 108 thousand trillion unique "lottery tickets" (i.e. actual, potential or notional human forenames), when the lottery is finally drawn, will be a winner (i.e. will be found to fall, purely by chance, into the centre of a complex web of patterns comparable to the **Pi Encryption**)?

20. We can answer that[(3)], very simply and certainly, by dividing the notional probability of success for any two numbers, regardless of whether or not they are linked to any particular name (i.e. 1: 1,350,200 x one trillion^{11}) by 108 thousand trillion (i.e. the total number of actual, potential or notional human forenames, which we are likening for this purpose to "lottery tickets" that have been sold, i.e. attempts, or chances of success, that can exist).

21. And the answer to that calculation is that the likelihood is well below **ONE CHANCE** in one trillion, trillion, trillion, trillion, trillion, trillion, trillion, trillion, trillion, trillion (one trillion to the power of ten)!

22. Yes, the probability of *any one* of the estimated 108 thousand trillion actual, potential or notional human forenames (*including* "Jesus") being found, by chance alone, to form the centre of a complex web of cryptic patterns equivalent to the

Pi Encryption, is certainly no higher than one chance in one trillion to the power of ten!

BUT WAIT, WE HAVEN'T FINISHED YET!

23. If (as we have seen above) the chance of *any one* human forename (*including* "Jesus") being found at the centre of a complex system of cryptic patterns such as the **Pi Encryption** is one chance in one trillion to the power of ten, then (given that, as we have seen in this book, the name "Jesus" is indeed to be found at the centre of just such a system of patterns), it must follow that the chance of *any second* name (one that is not "Jesus") *also* being found to be the centrepiece of an equivalent complex pattern system, is much, much, much smaller still.

24. And, applying exactly the same principles as we discussed, tossing coins, in the introduction to chapter 28, that chance can be calculated at one chance in one trillion^{10} x one trillion^{10} – in other words, one trillion to the power of ten multiplied by itself!

25. If one were to write this huge number out in full, it would be a 1, followed by 240 zeros – **roughly equivalent to the number of atoms in thirteen trillion universes!** (4)

26. Now, I hope you can fully understand why I answered "**YES**" to the question at the beginning of this Appendix, so boldly and with such absolute confidence.

27. **ON THE AVAILABLE EVIDENCE, WE CAN CONCLUDE, WITH TOTAL CONVICTION, (AND BEYOND ANY "REASONABLE DOUBT" WHATSOEVER) THAT "JESUS" IS THE ONLY NAME ENCRYPTED IN PI!**(5)

Notes on Appendix 11

(1) This figure of "just under 100 thousand trillion" is actually 99,246,114,928,149,462, and represents the total number of potential vocalisations of 12 or fewer letters which are capable of being represented by the 26 letters of the English alphabet, from the simplest single letter sounds (such as "a", "m", etc) to complex 12 letter combinations (such as the light-hearted and humorous examples given above - "Dribblychops", "Humptydumpty," "Cantankerous," "Haemorrhoids," "Zmkvbtcfhsqx" and kkkkkkkkkkkk").

As well as spawning many billions of never-used (and frankly unusable) potential forenames, we can be absolutely sure that, using this method, no forenames that have ever been used, or are ever capable of being used, are excluded, providing they do not exceed 12 letters in length.

The very small number of usable names that are excluded by this method (i.e. those with more than 12 letters) are more than adequately outnumbered by the huge number of those that have been included, because they have 12 or fewer letters, but which nevertheless are unused or unusable. For those who may be interested in checking them, I include the calculations in full below:

Vocalisations (i.e. potential forenames) containing:

1	letter	26
2	letters 26^2	676
3	letters 26^3	17,576
4	letters 26^4	456,976
5	letters 26^5	11,881,376
6	letters 26^6	308,915,776
7	letters 26^7	8,031,810,176
8	letters 26^8	208,827,064,576
9	letters 26^9	5,429,503,678,976
10	letters 26^{10}	141,167,095,653,376
11	letters 26^{11}	3,670,344,486,987,776
12	letters 26^{12}	95,428,956,661,682,176
	Total:	**99,246,114,928,149,462**

(2) The Population Reference Bureau, http://www.prb.org.

(3) If all ("Y") tickets are sold in a lottery, the chance of any particular one of them winning is 1:Y. If some ("Z") of the tickets are sold to a given group (such as university students, or people with ginger hair), the chance that any winning ticket was sold to a member of that group is 1:(Y/Z), and the chance that any two winning tickets were sold to members of that group is 1:[(Y/Z) x (Y/Z)]. Exactly the same principles apply to the matter under discussion, where 1:Y is the probability of a group of patterns, such as the Pi Encryption, forming randomly on the basis of any two numbers (such as 386 and 888) which may or may not relate to a particular forename, and "Z"

is the total number of theoretically possible forenames from which such an encryption could potentially be formed. If it is found (as it has been here) that a pair of numbers related to a particular forename (such as 386 and 888, which relate to the forename "Jesus") do indeed form the basis for such a group of patterns, the chance of this occurring is 1:(Y/Z); and the chance of any other pair of numbers related to a different forename also being found, on the basis of which such a group of patterns can form, is 1:[(Y/Z)x(Y/Z)].

(N.B. it has to be admitted that my methodology is slightly flawed at this point, in that a few of the features of the Pi Encryption are not based entirely on <u>386</u> and <u>888</u>, like the others, but, at least in part, on <u>86</u>. However, any slight distortion introduced by this is more than fully compensated for by the extremely conservative manner in which "Y" has been calculated – see chapter 27, "Stacking the Odds").

(4) According to science, it has been estimated (how reliably, I cannot say) that the total number of atoms in the observed universe is about 10^{80}, or a one with 80 zeros following it. This is called "the Eddington number" after the British astrophysicist Arthur Eddington (1882-1944). If this estimate is true, the figure calculated above (of a 1 followed by 240 zeros) would be roughly equivalent to the number of atoms in 13 trillion universes.

(5) Any forenames, other than "Jesus", that also fortuitously happened to have Hebrew and Greek numerical values of "386" and "888", (if they existed), would also be swept into the encryption, but of course this is both inevitable and immaterial to the point under discussion.

www.ingramcontent.com/pod-product-compliance
Lightning Source LLC
LaVergne TN
LVHW050344210926
848481LV00017B/1454
9781068338410